Service Assessment

Hurricane Katrina
August 23-31, 2005

June 2006

NOAA's National Weather Service
David L. Johnson
Brigadier General, USAF (ret.)
Assistant Administrator for Weather Services

National Oceanic and Atmospheric Administration
Weather Bureau Hurricane Series

ERRATA NOTICE

One or more conditions of the original document may affect the quality of the image, such as:

Discolored pages
Faded or light ink
Binding intrudes into the text

This has been a co-operative project between the NOAA Central Library and the Climate Database Modernization Program, National Climate Data Center (NCDC). To view the original document contact the NOAA Central Library in Silver Spring, MD at (301) 713-2607 x124 or Library.Reference@noaa.gov.

HOV Services
Imaging Contractor
12200 Kiln Court
Beltsville, MD 20704-1387
November 6, 2007

Preface

The devastation along the Gulf Coast from Hurricane Katrina was staggering. The physical destruction and personal suffering surmounted that of any U.S. weather disaster in recent history. The loss of life and extraordinary damage made Katrina the costliest hurricane in U.S. history and one of the five deadliest hurricanes to ever strike the U.S. However, without NOAA's National Weather Service forecasts, warnings, communication, outreach, and education, the impacts and loss of life would have been far greater.

I chartered a team to assess NWS performance during the event. The Team found the NWS performed exceptionally well in forecasting, warning, communication, preparedness, and post-storm recovery efforts. This is confirmed by the overwhelming positive response received from users and partners of the NWS.

Our National Hurricane Center predicted the central Gulf Coast, including the New Orleans metropolitan area, would be directly affected by Katrina as a major hurricane about 56 hours before landfall. Forecasts of Katrina's path from NHC were better than long-term average errors and better than the Government Performance and Results Act (GPRA) 2006 goals established for hurricane track forecasts.

The evacuation rate during Hurricane Katrina was near 80 percent. This is an impressive public response to an approaching threat. This remarkable response resulted from a long-working relationship and open communication between NWS, the emergency management community at all levels, and the media.

While NOAA's National Weather Service performed well in forecasts and services, there is room for improvement. The Assessment Team made 16 recommendations, most of which concern the infrastructure of the NWS such as electrical power, communications, computing systems, and data gathering systems. During extremely difficult working conditions, the ingenuity, dedication, and sheer will of NWS employees enabled the provision of products and services as infrastructure and back-up systems failed. Relying on NWS employees to overcome infrastructure failure is not an ideal solution. The recommendations in this report will be addressed and the 13 best practices will be considered nationwide.

David L. Johnson
Brigadier General, USAF (Ret.)
Assistant Administrator for Weather Services
June 2006

Table of Contents

Preface... ii

Service Assessment Team... iv

Acknowledgements.. v

Acronyms.. vi

Executive Summary 1

Service Assessment Report

Introduction... 4

Event Overview 5

NWS Forecast and Warning Services.. 9

    National Centers for Environmental Prediction... 9
    Florida Weather Forecast Offices 15
    Gulf Coast Weather Forecast Offices 16

Operations Coordination.. 23

Continuity of Operations.. 26

Support Activities 32

Outreach and Preparedness.. 34

Best Practices.. 36

Conclusion 37

Appendices

The Saffir-Simpson Hurricane Scale A-1

Best Track Analysis for Hurricane Katrina B-1

Tornado Reports Associated with Hurricane Katrina.. C-1

Service Assessment Team

This Service Assessment Team was assembled on September 9, 2005 and initially convened at the National Centers for Environmental Prediction's Tropical Prediction Center on September 12-13, 2005. The Team conducted 20 NWS field office visits/reviews over a six-week period to evaluate NWS performance during Katrina. During its field office visits, the Team met with more than 40 representatives from the emergency management community and the mass media. The Team was comprised the following individuals:

John L. Guiney   *Team Leader*, Chief, Meteorological Services Division, NWS Eastern Region Headquarters (ERH), Bohemia, New York

Curtis D. Carey   NWS Communications Office, NWS Headquarters, Silver Spring, Maryland

Dennis M. Decker   Warning Coordination Meteorologist, Weather Forecast Office (WFO) Melbourne, Florida

Lew Fincher   Vice President, Hurricane Consulting, Inc., Friendswood, Texas

William J. Gery   NWS Systems Manager, NWS Central Region Headquarters, Kansas City, Missouri

Scott C. Kiser   NWS Tropical Cyclone Program Leader, Office of Climate, Water, and Weather Services (OCWWS), NWS Headquarters, Silver Spring, Maryland

Steven Piltz   Meteorologist-in-Charge, WFO Tulsa, Oklahoma

Anthony Siebers   Meteorologist-in-Charge, WFO Wakefield, Virginia

Larry Vannozzi   Meteorologist-in-Charge, WFO Nashville, Tennessee

Other valuable contributors include:

Laurie G. Hogan   Hydrometeorologist, NWS ERH, Bohemia, New York

Billy Olsen   Hydrologist-in-Charge, Arkansas-Red Basin River Forecast Center, Tulsa, Oklahoma

Aimee Devaris   Chief, Performance Branch, OCWWS, NWS Headquarters, Silver Spring, Maryland

Wayne Presnell   National Service Assessment Program Leader, OCWWS, NWS Headquarters, Silver Spring, Maryland

Acknowledgements

The team would like to thank our partners in emergency management, the media, and individuals from all of the NWS offices who took time to talk and share their thoughts and experiences with us. We would also like to acknowledge NOAA's National Environmental Satellite, Data, and Information Service (NESDIS); all of the satellite images used in this report are courtesy of NESDIS.

The Team is also grateful to the following individuals for reviewing portions of the document and for suggestions that improved the report: Peter Gabrielsen, Heather Hauser, Mickey Brown, Theodore Wilk, and Hector Machado. We also appreciate the assistance of Richard Watling with tornado statistics and Donald J. Miller III, who assisted with data analysis for the Lower Mississippi River Forecast Center backup review.

Acronyms

ASOS	Automated Surface Observing System
AHPS	Advanced Hydrologic Prediction System
AWIPS	Advanced Weather Information Processing System
BLM	Bureau of Land Management
CDT	Central Daylight Time
C-MAN	Coastal Marine Automated Network
CWSU	Center Weather Service Unit
DART	Deep-ocean Assessment and Reporting of Tsunami [buoy station]
EDT	Eastern Daylight Time
EOC	Emergency Operations Center
FEMA	Federal Emergency Management Agency
GHG	Graphical Hazards Generator [software]
HSOC	Homeland Security Operations Center
HLS	Hurricane Local Statement
HLT	Hurricane Liaison Team
HPC	Hydrometeorological Prediction Center
HURRTRAK	Hurricane tracking software
IMET	Incident Meteorologist
Knots	Nautical Miles per hour (1 knot equal to 1.15 mph)
LEOC	Louisiana Emergency Operations Center
LHSOC	Louisiana Homeland Security Operations Center
mb	Millibar
MEMA	Mississippi Emergency Management Agency
mph	Miles per hour
NASA	National Aeronautics and Space Administration
NCEP	National Centers for Environmental Prediction
NDFD	National Digital Forecast Database
NHC	National Hurricane Center
nm	Nautical miles
NOAA	National Oceanic and Atmospheric Administration
NDBC	National Data Buoy Center
NWR	NOAA Weather Radio All Hazards
NWS	National Weather Service
NWSH	National Weather Service Headquarters
OCWWS	Office of Climate, Water, and Weather Services
RAWS	Remote Automated Weather Station
ROC	Regional Operations Center
RFC	River Forecast Center
SAT	Service Assessment Team
SLOSH	Sea Lake and Overland Surges from Hurricanes
SPC	Storm Prediction Center
SRH	Southern Region Headquarters
TCM	Tropical Cyclone Marine Advisory
TPC	Tropical Prediction Center

TPC/NHC	Tropical Prediction Center/National Hurricane Center
TOR	Tornado [communications identifier/code]
USACE	United States Army Corps of Engineers
WAN	Wide Area Network
WFO	Weather Forecast Office
WGRFC	Western Gulf River Forecast Center
WSR-88D	Weather Service Radar, 1988 Doppler
WWA	Watch, Warning, Advisory [software]

Executive Summary

After crossing South Florida and gaining strength over the Gulf of Mexico, the center of Hurricane Katrina made landfall in southeast Louisiana at 6:10 a.m. local time on August 29. Katrina was then a large Category 3 hurricane (See **Appendix A** for Saffir-Simpson Scale) with winds of 125 mph and a central pressure of 920 millibars (mb). This makes Katrina the third most intense United States (U.S.) land-falling hurricane on record based on central pressure. Katrina's center moved ashore near the Louisiana and Mississippi border around 9:45 a.m. and continued to move north through Mississippi, maintaining hurricane intensity almost 100 miles inland. Over the next two days, Katrina moved north through the lower Mississippi Valley into the Ohio River Valley region, spreading destructive winds well inland and spawning dozens of tornadoes.

The devastation left in Katrina's wake over southeast Louisiana and coastal Mississippi was immense. The storm surge ravaged coastal Mississippi, and several levee breaches occurred in and around New Orleans. The levee breaches and overtopping resulted in floodwaters of 15 to 20 feet covering about 80 percent of the city. The catastrophic damage and loss of life inflicted by this hurricane is staggering, with an estimated 1,353 direct fatalities[1] and 275,000 homes damaged or destroyed. According to the American Insurance Services Group, Katrina caused an estimated $40.6 billion in insured losses (as of June 2006). The National Hurricane Center (NHC) typically doubles the estimated insured losses for an estimate of total damage losses in the U.S., giving an estimated total $81.2 billion in damage. Total economic losses could be greater than $100 billion. These impacts make Katrina the costliest hurricane in U.S. history and one of the five deadliest hurricanes to ever strike the U.S.

Tens of thousands of jobs were lost due to severely damaged or destroyed businesses and supporting infrastructure. Major highways in and around New Orleans were damaged or destroyed, disrupting commerce. Katrina also affected the oil and gas industry by damaging platforms and shutting down refineries, and interrupted operations at two major U.S. ports in Louisiana.

While NWS offices were heavily engaged in forecast and warning operations during Katrina, the impacts of the storm created extremely challenging working and living conditions. Katrina caused significant disruptions in the communication infrastructure in southeast Louisiana. As a result, the NWS offices in Louisiana and Mississippi experienced communications outages affecting their ability to monitor weather conditions and disseminate forecasts, warnings, and information. Continuity of operations plans (COOP) were implemented for each of the impacted NWS offices in Louisiana and Mississippi. Under these plans, NWS offices from Texas to Florida were involved in providing the necessary backup services.

---

[1] This estimate, as of May 15, 2006, is based on information from affected states' Departments of Health. The total includes direct fatalities only and does not include out of state evacuee fatalities included in some calculations. Fatalities by state: Louisiana, 1097, Mississippi, 238, Florida 14, Alabama 2, and Georgia 2.

The support effort of NWS Incident Meteorologists (IMET) was substantial and successful during Katrina. IMETs provide tactical and logistical weather information in support of a mission, such as clean up efforts after a major weather-related disaster. The hurricane disabled or destroyed weather sensors across the region. IMETs dispatched from other areas of the country, helped install temporary replacement equipment to monitor local weather conditions, including at New Orleans International Airport. They also provided briefings and forecasts for emergency responders and worked shifts for the WFO's local employees so they could begin to get their lives back in order after Katrina.

Due to the magnitude of the impacts of Hurricane Katrina, the NWS assembled a Service Assessment Team (SAT) to review the performance of its offices during the event. NWS service assessments are routinely conducted to identify and share best-case operations, procedures, and practices and address service deficiencies. The SAT evaluated the effectiveness of NWS services and operational procedures relating to the agency's performance with respect to this event, paying particular attention to continuity of operations procedures/plans, coordination and collaboration with emergency managers and other decision makers, and forecast and warning accuracy.

The SAT found that the NWS performed admirably, before, during, and after Katrina. Overall, the timeliness and accuracy of the forecast products and warnings issued by the NHC were well above average and contributed significantly to critical customer decision-making. The hurricane forecast track error was considerably better than average through the five-day forecast period. Lead times on hurricane watches and warnings for Louisiana, Mississippi, Alabama, and the Florida panhandle were eight hours above average. The overall intensity forecast error for Katrina was larger than average; however, the intensity forecasts within 48 to 72 hours of landfall in southeast Louisiana correctly projected Katrina as a major hurricane (Category 3 or higher). The largest errors were associated with the rapid intensification of Katrina over the open eastern Gulf of Mexico.

Throughout the event, NWS field offices provided high quality information to the public, mass media, and emergency management officials. **A noteworthy moment for the NWS came when the Weather Forecast Office (WFO) in New Orleans/Baton Rouge issued a statement one day prior to Katrina's landfall that emphasized the likely impacts of the hurricane on southeast Louisiana and coastal Mississippi. Due to the unprecedented detail and foreboding nature of the language used, the statement helped reinforce the actions of emergency management officials as they coordinated one of the largest evacuations in U.S. history.**

Service backup for offices affected by the communications outages was effective and transparent to most users and partners. However, the SAT noted several opportunities for improvement. Single points of failure in the commercial telecommunications system upon which the NWS relies in operations need to be identified and mitigated to improve continuity of operations plans for NWS field offices. The NWS should also explore an alternative communications system for NWS field offices to provide redundancy. Hardware and software requirements for extended periods of service backup support must be identified and addressed. Equipment failures and interruptions in power and/or communications also affected the availability of real-time weather observations during Katrina.

Both the emergency management and mass media communities indicated that the NWS provided excellent products and services during Katrina. However, feedback was mixed on one of the NWS's newest products, the Extreme Tropical Cyclone Destructive Wind Warning. Outreach activities on tropical weather services should focus on this issue to educate users about this product and communicate planned future changes to its format and/or content.

The NWS conducts routine service assessments to cultivate continuous performance improvement. The SAT reviewed the operations of 20 field offices to evaluate NWS performance during Katrina and gathered feedback from more than 40 members of the natural hazards community. This report provides specific recommendations and highlights best practices to be applied to NWS operations in future hazardous events.

Service Assessment Report

INTRODUCTION

The mission of NOAA's NWS is to save lives, mitigate property loss, and enhance the national economy. In the tropical cyclone program, this is accomplished through the issuance of timely and accurate tropical cyclone information (including watches, warnings, and forecasts) year round, especially during the Atlantic hurricane season (June 1 to November 30), as well as conducting an aggressive tropical cyclone outreach and preparedness campaign. The NWS continually partners with the Federal Emergency Management Agency (FEMA), other federal agencies, state, county/parish, and local emergency management agencies and officials, and the media to promote hurricane awareness and preparedness in tropical cyclone-prone areas of the United States. These relationships become especially important during tropical cyclone landfalls when it is critical to identify hazards and potential impacts.

The damage and loss of life inflicted by Hurricane Katrina was catastrophic. As of May 15, 2006, there have been an estimated 1,353 direct deaths due to Katrina, 275,000 homes were damaged or destroyed, and insured damage estimates are $40.6 billion according to the American Insurance Services Group (as of June 2006). These impacts make Katrina the costliest hurricane in U.S. history and one of the five deadliest hurricanes to ever strike the U.S.

Economic impacts from Hurricane Katrina were also considerable. Tens of thousands of jobs were lost due to severely damaged or destroyed businesses and supporting infrastructure. Major highways in and around New Orleans were damaged or destroyed, disrupting commerce. Katrina had a profound impact on the southeast Louisiana/Mississippi oil and gas industry, which accounts for nearly 30 percent of total domestic crude and 20 percent of domestic natural gas production. More than 30 oil platforms were damaged or destroyed and nine refineries were damaged and/or shut down for weeks following the storm. The hurricane also disrupted operations at the Port of South Louisiana and the Port of New Orleans, the first and fifth largest ports in the U.S., respectively. Together, these ports account for $150 billion and 20 percent of U.S. import/export cargo traffic annually.

As a result of the devastating impact of Katrina, the NWS chartered and assembled a Service Assessment Team (SAT). The NWS service assessment process is an evaluative learning tool designed to identify and share operational best practices and procedures and address service deficiencies. The SAT was responsible for evaluating the performance of the NWS and making recommendations for improving NWS services and operations.

The SAT conducted 20 NWS field office visits/reviews over a six-week period. In addition, the SAT gathered feedback from more than 40 members of the hazard community. This report provides an overview of the hydrometeorological aspects of Katrina, NWS forecast and warning services, continuity of operations activities, coordination, outreach and preparedness, and post-storm support and response. In

4

addition to documenting 13 best practices, the SAT identified opportunities for service improvement in 16 findings and recommendations.

EVENT OVERVIEW

On August 19, Katrina developed north of Puerto Rico from a combination of a tropical wave and the remnants of Tropical Depression Ten. Atmospheric conditions became more conducive for development and the system became a tropical depression on August 23 about 175 miles southeast of Nassau in the Bahamas. On August 24, the system continued to organize and was named "Tropical Storm Katrina" while moving northwest through the Bahamas. Katrina then turned west toward South Florida and continued to strengthen, reaching Category 1 hurricane strength less than two hours before its initial U.S. landfall near the Miami-Dade and Broward County line during the evening of August 25 (**Figure 1**).

On August 26, Katrina moved onshore in South Florida as a Category 1 hurricane and weakened to a tropical storm while over land. As the center moved across Miami-Dade County, the eye passed directly over the building housing NHC and WFO Miami. Katrina strengthened again to a Category 1 hurricane later that day when it moved over the eastern Gulf of Mexico. Continuing its southwest movement, Katrina intensified to a Category 2 hurricane by 11:30 a.m. Eastern Daylight Time (EDT) on August 26.

Figure 1. NWS WSR-88D radar image of Katrina making landfall in South Florida at 6:30 p.m. EDT August 25, 2005.

From 1 p.m. CDT August 26 to 1 p.m. CDT August 28, Katrina's central pressure dropped from 968 mb to its lowest pressure of 902 mb, a drop of 66 mb in 48 hours. Katrina's maximum sustained winds increased from an estimated 95 mph to an estimated 175 mph during this same period, making Katrina a Category 5 hurricane while it was centered about 170 miles southeast of the mouth of the Mississippi River. This makes Katrina the sixth most intense hurricane (based on central pressure) on record in the

Atlantic basin (**Table 1**). The greatest central pressure drop in an Atlantic Basin hurricane occurred in Hurricane Gilbert in September 1988. Its central pressure dropped 72 mb in 24 hours and its maximum sustained winds increased from an estimated 125 mph to an estimated 185 mph. **Figure 2** is a satellite image of Katrina near peak intensity on August 28.

HURRICANE	YEAR	MINIMUM PRESSURE
Hurricane Wilma	2005	882 mb
Hurricane Gilbert	1988	888 mb
The Labor Day Hurricane	1935	892 mb
Hurricane Rita	2005	895 mb
Hurricane Allen	1980	899 mb
Hurricane Katrina	2005	902 mb
Hurricane Camille	1969	905 mb
Hurricane Mitch	1998	905 mb
Hurricane Ivan	2004	910 mb
Hurricane Janet	1955	914 mb

Table 1. The ten most intense hurricanes (based on central pressure) in the Atlantic basin 1851-2005.

On August 28, Katrina made a gradual turn toward the northwest and north toward the central Gulf of Mexico coast. During this period, Katrina's wind field expanded considerably with hurricane-force winds extending about 125 miles from the center and tropical storm-force winds 230 miles from the center.

Figure 2. NOAA-16 satellite image of Katrina at 3:11 p.m. Central Daylight Time (CDT) August 28, 2005 near peak intensity (minimum central pressure 902 mb, maximum sustained winds 175 mph).

At 6:10 a.m. Central Daylight Time (CDT) August 29, the center of Katrina made landfall in Plaquemines Parish, LA, just south of Buras, as a Category 3 hurricane with estimated maximum sustained winds near 125 mph and a minimum central pressure of

920 mb. This is the third lowest central pressure of a land-falling hurricane in the U.S. (**Table 2**).

HURRICANE	YEAR	MINIMUM PRESSURE AT LANDFALL
Labor Day Hurricane (FL Keys)	1935	892 mb
Hurricane Camille (SE LA/MS)	1969	909 mb
Hurricane Katrina (SE LA/MS)	2005	920 mb
Hurricane Andrew (SE FL)	1992	922 mb
Indianola (TX)	1919	925 mb

Table 2. The five most intense hurricanes (based on central pressure) to make landfall in the U.S. 1851-2005.

Katrina then moved ashore near the Louisiana and Mississippi border around 9:45 a.m. CDT as a Category 3 hurricane with estimated sustained winds of 120 mph and a minimum central pressure of 928 mb. Katrina weakened to a tropical storm by 7 p.m. CDT, August 29, while located just north of Laurel, MS. Over the next two days, the storm moved north through the lower Mississippi Valley into the Ohio River Valley region spreading destructive winds and spawning tornadoes. Katrina was downgraded to a tropical depression near Clarksville, TN, on August 30 and was absorbed by a frontal system in southeastern Canada on the night of August 31. **Appendix B** provides Katrina's best track analysis from TPC/NHC.

Katrina produced 62 tornadoes in eight states from Florida to Pennsylvania (**Appendix C**). The average lead-time for NWS tornado warnings during Katrina was 12 minutes. The highest rainfall total recorded in Katrina was 16.33 inches in Perrine, FL; Big Branch, LA, recorded 14.92 inches of rainfall, the highest rainfall amount in Louisiana.

The highest measured wind gust during Katrina was 135 mph, recorded in Popularville, MS, at Pearl River County Emergency Operations Center (EOC) before the instrument failed. Katrina produced wind gusts of 80 to 110 mph well inland over portions of southern, central, and eastern Mississippi. The highest reported wind gust in inland Mississippi was 114 mph in Ellisville. The strongest official sustained wind in Louisiana during Katrina was 87 mph measured at the Grand Isle Coastal Marine Automated Network (C-MAN) station. This station failed two hours before the eye passed nearby. The lowest observed pressure was 920.2 mb at the University of Louisiana - Monroe Weather Station in Buras, LA.

Storm surge data indicates that the maximum surge was 26 to 28 feet along the coast of Mississippi. Damage survey data suggests that the surge penetrated at least six miles inland in many portions of coastal Mississippi. The estimated storm surge in southeast Louisiana near New Orleans was 10 to 15 feet and 10 to 12 feet along the coast of Alabama. Four levee breaches occurred around New Orleans on August 29: two along the London Avenue Canal, one along the 17th Street Canal, and one along the Industrial Canal. **Figure 3** shows the locations where the breaches occurred.

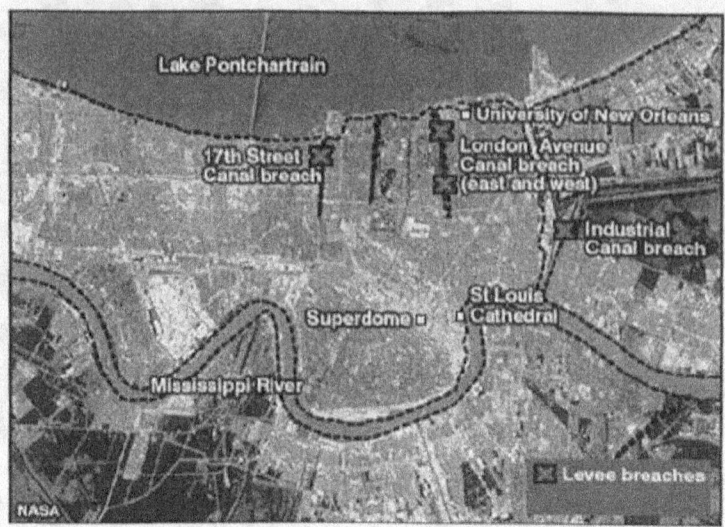

Figure 3. Levee breaches in New Orleans during Katrina.
Courtesy of the National Aeronautics and Space Administration (NASA)

  The floodwaters from the Industrial Canal levee breach submerged much of the Lower Ninth Ward and areas nearby, including St. Bernard Parish, trapping thousands of people on rooftops and in attics. The 17th Street Canal breach resulted in a slow-rising flood over a larger area. Several levees around New Orleans were overtopped adding to the flooding problems. Data from the U.S. Army Corps of Engineers (USACE) indicates that the breaches and overtopped levees flooded approximately 80 percent of the city to varying depths, with floodwaters approaching 20 feet in some places (**Figure 4**). Hurricane Rita affected the area a few weeks later, delaying the removal of the floodwaters. The USACE finished removing all floodwaters from New Orleans on October 11, 43 days after Katrina's landfall.

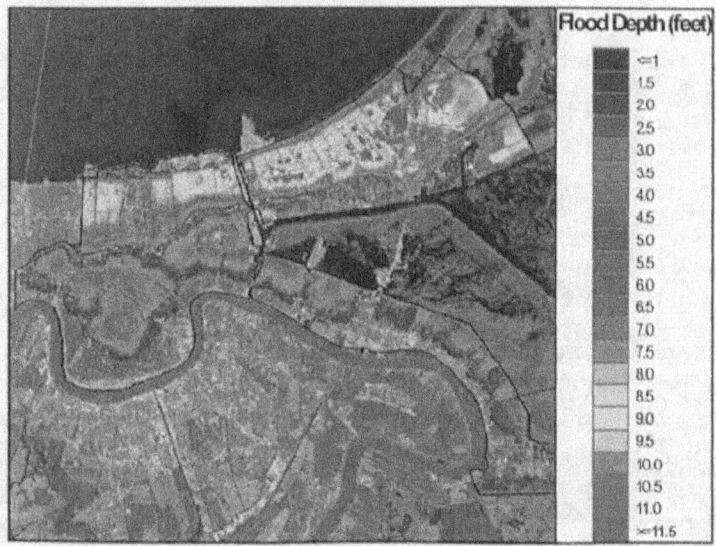

Figure 4. Estimated water depth in feet for flooded areas of New Orleans on September 2, 2005. Areas in bright red indicate depths over 11.5 feet. Courtesy of the U.S. Geological Survey.

(a)   (b)

Figure 5. Images of flooding in New Orleans, LA: (a) Canal Street on the morning of August 31; (b) A view from the air looking into the city from the east with Claiborne Avenue Bridge in the back left and the Judge Seber Bridge in the back right on September 6, 2005. *Courtesy of the New Orleans Times Picayune*

NWS FORECAST AND WARNING SERVICES

NWS forecast and warning services are provided through the collaborative efforts of a number of offices with unique areas of expertise and responsibility. Several offices within the National Centers for Environmental Prediction (NCEP) work closely with the WFOs, River Forecast Centers (RFC), and Center Weather Service Units (CWSU) to coordinate the issuance and discontinuance of watches and warnings and discuss storm surge forecasts, flood potential, and other storm parameters such as effects on aviation. This collaboration also extends to the emergency management community through the Hurricane Liaison Team (HLT).

The HLT is a Department of Homeland Security/FEMA-sponsored team made up of NOAA/NWS employees and federal, state, and local emergency managers and who have extensive hurricane operational experience. The director of the National Hurricane Center (NHC) can request HLT activation whenever tropical storms threaten. Team members function as a bridge between scientists, meteorologists and the emergency managers who respond if the storm threatens the U.S. or its territories. Team members provide immediate and critical storm information to government agency decision-makers at all levels to help them prepare for their response operations, which may include evacuations, sheltering, and mobilizing equipment.

National Centers for Environmental Prediction

NCEP delivers global and national weather, water, climate and space weather guidance, forecasts, warnings, and analyses to a broad range of users and partners via its nine service centers. These service centers include the Hydrometeorological Prediction Center (HPC), the Storm Prediction Center (SPC), and the National Hurricane Center/Tropical Prediction Center (NHC/TPC). The products and services produced by these service centers support the NWS mission.

Storm Prediction Center

The SPC provides forecasts and watches for severe thunderstorms and tornadoes over the contiguous United States. The SPC also monitors heavy rain, heavy snow, and fire weather events across the United States and issues specific products for those hazards. During the Atlantic hurricane season, SPC collaborates with NHC on the potential tornado threat for land-falling tropical cyclones. This is accomplished in several ways. SPC provides its input to NHC regarding the potential for tornadoes, and tornado watch issuances, during internal Hurricane Hotline coordination calls. Once a tornado threat for a tropical cyclone exists, SPC becomes a participant on a NOAA/FEMA led HLT. The HLT provides information on land-falling tropical systems in the U.S. for FEMA senior leadership and state emergency management officials.

NHC included the first statement regarding the potential for isolated tornadoes with Katrina in the public advisory on August 25. During Katrina's landfall in South Florida, no tornado watch was issued. A single tornado was reported in the Florida Keys. On August 27, TPC/NHC removed the threat of tornadoes from the public advisory as Katrina moved away from the Florida Keys. On the morning of August 28, TPC/NHC, in consultation with SPC, issued a new threat area for tornadoes with Katrina in the public advisory:

> *ISOLATED TORNADOES WILL BE POSSIBLE BEGINNING SUNDAY EVENING OVER SOUTHERN PORTIONS OF LOUISIANA...MISSISSIPPI...AND ALABAMA...AND OVER THE FLORIDA PANHANDLE.*

SPC began to provide information regarding the tornado threat associated with Katrina across portions of the north central and northeast coast of the Gulf of Mexico on HLT calls on August 28. They issued 10 tornado watches in the south and east central United States as Katrina moved inland. Sixty-one tornadoes occurred from August 28 to August 30 from Mississippi to Pennsylvania.

Hydrometeorological Prediction Center (HPC)

The HPC provides forecasts, guidance, and analysis products and services to support NWS and other government agencies with daily public forecasting activities. During the Atlantic hurricane season, HPC provides real-time track guidance for all tropical cyclones west of 60° longitude (about 400 miles east of Puerto Rico) to support the NWS tropical cyclone forecast and warning program. In addition, HPC provides the precipitation statements for all NHC-issued public advisories. Once a tropical cyclone moves inland and NHC discontinues advisories, HPC assumes responsibility for monitoring the system. HPC public advisories include information regarding the system's position over land, intensity, general forecast trends, observed conditions, and impacts (usually in relation to heavy rain/flooding and tornadoes). HPC public advisories are discontinued when the threat of river and flash flooding has ended.

10

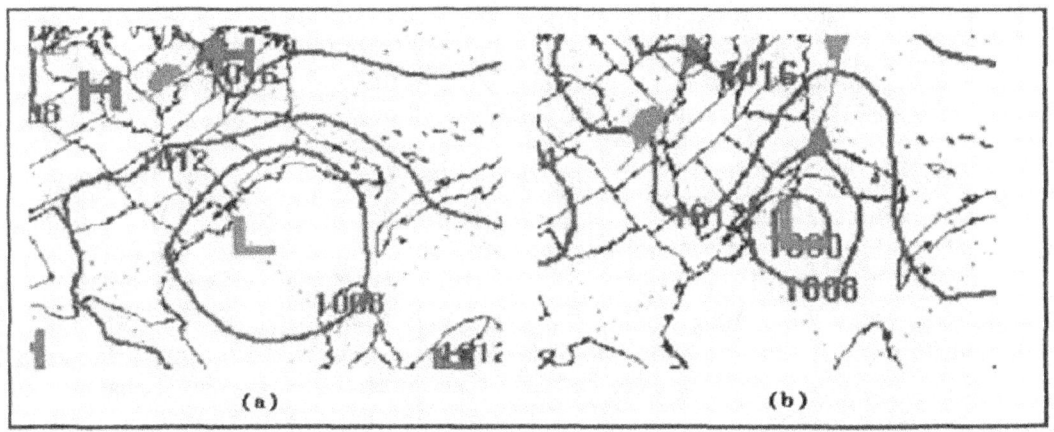

Figure 6. HPC forecasts valid for Monday, August 29, 2005 issued six and seven days in advance of Katrina. (a) The Day 7 forecast issued on Monday, August 22, 2005; (b) The Day 6 forecast position issued on Tuesday, August 23, 2005.

During the hurricane season, NHC and HPC collaborate daily on tropical cyclone features for the day 6-7 forecast period. NHC and HPC initially identified the system that was to become Katrina on August 22. Subsequently, this system was placed on the HPC Day 7 forecast surface pressure map in the north central Gulf of Mexico just south of New Orleans, LA, valid August 29. The following day, HPC continued to forecast a system in the northeast Gulf of Mexico on the Day 6 forecast surface pressure map (**Figure 6**).

On August 24, HPC began preparing rainfall statements for NHC public advisories on Katrina. On August 25, HPC became a participant in HLT briefings for Katrina. HPC's portion of the briefings covered the precipitation forecast for Katrina. At 4 p.m. CDT August 30, HPC assumed responsibility for issuing public advisories for Katrina. HPC discontinued advisories for Katrina on the night of August 31, as the system was absorbed by a frontal system over the eastern Great Lakes.

One of HPC's most critical functions is performing service backup for NHC. HPC has been aggressive in maintaining proficiency on NHC service backup requirements. This included conducting several backup drills during June and July 2005. Recently, they have also expanded the pool of forecasters involved in service backup responsibilities that provides HPC with additional resources and flexibility (**Best Practice**). HPC has designated a tropical cyclone training focal point who develops a training plan to support HPC's tropical cyclone responsibilities, including backup functions.

Tropical Prediction Center

TPC provides forecast, warning, guidance, and analysis products and services for tropical systems extending from the west coast of Africa to just east of Hawaii. TPC is composed of three branches: the Tropical Analysis and Forecast branch (TAFB), the Technical Support Branch (TSB), and the NHC. NHC provides operational tropical cyclone outlooks, forecasts, watches, and warnings for the Atlantic and Northeast Pacific basins. During the Atlantic hurricane season, TAFB provides Dvorak satellite tropical cyclone position and intensity estimates to support TPC/NHC operations, while TSB provides operational support for the SLOSH (Sea, Lake, and Overland Surges from Hurricanes) storm surge model and maintains TPC Information Technology equipment. Both TAFB and TSB also assist with TPC/NHC operations.

NHC's overall performance during Katrina was excellent. The NHC forecasts provided a consistent message regarding the forecast track and intensity of Katrina. NHC forecasts and discussions were timely, and they effectively conveyed the level of confidence in the forecast which enhanced the utility of NWS information during this event. NHC forecasts allowed WFOs to provide timely and accurate local information and advise emergency managers of potential threats and impacts of Katrina. NHC also provided several unscheduled updates that kept users informed on important changes and trends following a recommendation from the Hurricane Charley service assessment report. A broadcast meteorologist in Mississippi acknowledged this service as being particularly helpful and appreciated.

NHC's official track forecasts for Katrina issued within about two and a half days of landfall in Louisiana were exceptionally accurate and consistent. The forecast errors were considerably less than the average official Atlantic track errors for the 10-year period 1995-2004. Every official forecast that was issued beginning at 5 p.m. EDT on August 26 showed a track crossing the coast of Mississippi and/or southeastern Louisiana. The NHC does not explicitly issue forecasts for the precise location or timing of landfall. The official track forecasts issued 12, 24, 36, and 48 hours prior to 8 a.m. August 29 were in error by only 19, 24, 32, and 56 nautical miles, respectively, an improvement of 31 to 44 percent over the corresponding average track errors for 1995-2004. These errors are less than half the magnitude of the corresponding 10-year averages (1995-2004) among all Atlantic basin forecasts. Meanwhile, the track errors for the 72 to 120 hour periods were somewhat higher but still 10 to 25 percent below the average errors for the past five years. The relatively small errors at 12-48 hours greatly helped in the issuance of accurate and timely coastal watches and warnings.

The lead time for hurricane watches and warnings for South Florida were 32 hours and 20 hours, slightly below the 36 hour and 24 hour targets, but the lead times for southeast Louisiana of 44 hours and 32 hours were excellent. Moreover, the TPC/NHC forecast at 11 p.m. EDT August 26, showed Katrina making landfall as a major hurricane – a full 56 hours before landfall (see **Figure 7**).

Average official intensity forecast errors during Katrina were between 10 to 28 knots for the 12 to 48 hour forecast period, and between 36 to 47 knots for the 72 to 120 hour forecast periods. These errors were considerably larger than the corresponding Atlantic 10-year (1995-2004) averages. Despite the larger than average intensity errors, the official forecasts provided some important information, with respect to the issued watches and warnings, of what the intensity could be at the initial U.S. landfall in Florida. Additionally, every official forecast within about three days of landfall in Louisiana correctly anticipated that Katrina would be a major hurricane (at least Category 3) at landfall on the northern Gulf coast. Katrina was an unusually intense hurricane and underwent two rapid intensification periods, including the very rapid strengthening from

Category 3 to Category 5 on the morning of August 28. Accurately forecasting the timing and magnitude of such extreme hurricanes remains an operational challenge.

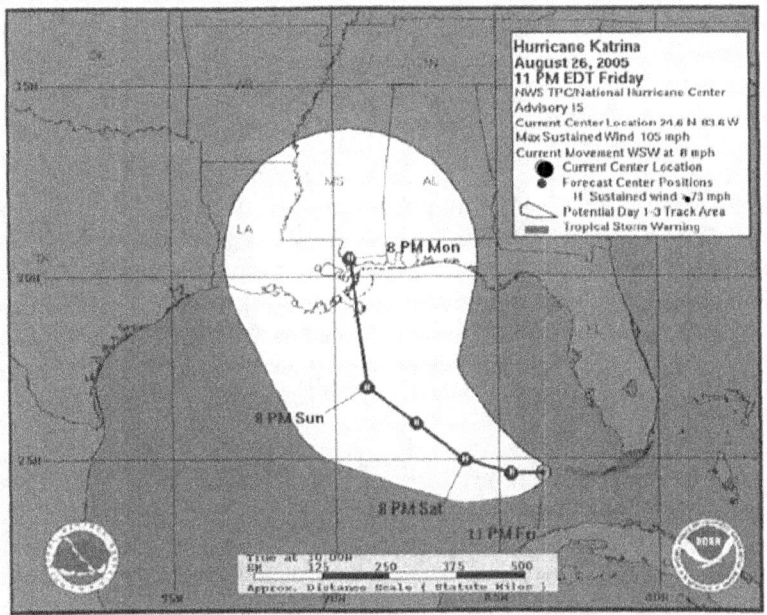

Figure 7. NHC 72 hour hurricane forecast issued at 11 p.m. EDT August 26 – 56 hours prior to Katrina's landfall in southeast Louisiana. The cone of uncertainty is represented by the white shading.

According to Louisiana emergency management, it takes 48 to 72 hours to evacuate vulnerable residents from New Orleans. NHC's forecasts afforded emergency management and the public 56 hours to implement their hurricane plans and make evacuation decisions along the north central Gulf Coast.

One of the challenges TPC/NHC encountered during Katrina was projecting the path of the storm across South Florida and the Florida Keys (**Figure 8**). Katrina moved southwest as it passed over the southern Florida peninsula, south of original forecast track but within historic 10-year average track errors. The more southerly track resulted in tropical storm-force and hurricane-force winds in the lower Florida Keys and a three to five foot storm surge in portions of Monroe County. There was adequate watch and warning time for the Florida Keys, but a watch was not posted for the Dry Tortugas. TPC/NHC issued a tropical storm warning for the Dry Tortugas at 1 a.m. EDT, August 26, but no hurricane warning was issued. An observation platform there reported tropical storm force winds for about 26 hours beginning about 11 a.m. EDT on August 26, and hurricane force winds were reported for one hour during that period.

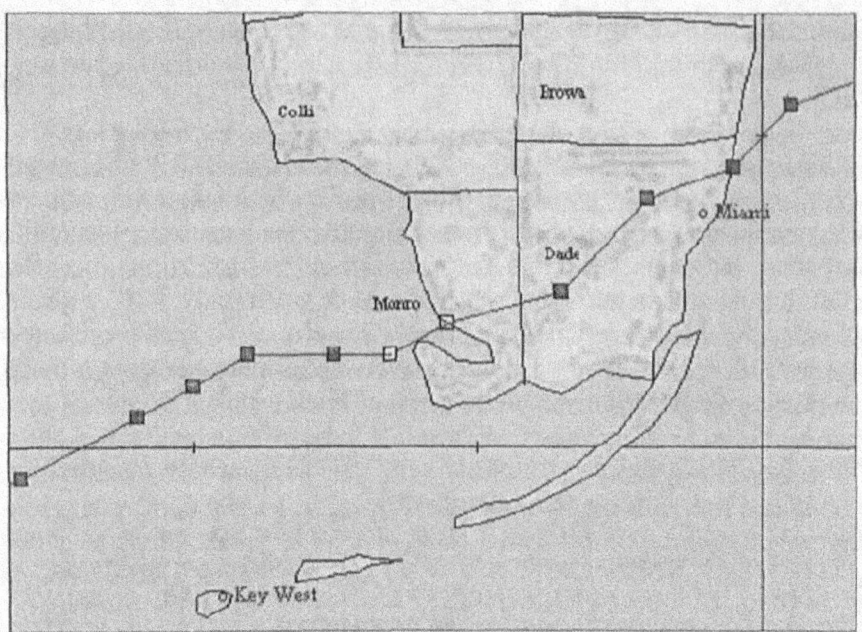

Figure 8. Locations of Katrina's center of circulation as it moved across south Florida between 5 p.m. August 25 and 11 pm August 26. Courtesy of WFO Miami. Yellow boxes denote tropical storm strength and red denote hurricane.

The 4 p.m. EDT August 26 advisory issued by TPC/NHC shifted the track of Katrina about 150 nautical miles to the west into the north-central coast of the Gulf of Mexico. In the same advisory, TPC/NHC also indicated that Katrina would reach Category 4 status. This forecast of aggressive strengthening was supported by three computer guidance models, which, when cited in the forecast discussion, provided increased confidence for the strengthening trend.

The final significant adjustment to the TPC/NHC forecast occurred in the 10 p.m. CDT, August 26 advisory, 56 hours before landfall. The track was adjusted farther west to project a landfall in southeast Louisiana and a second landfall near the Louisiana/Mississippi border, and the intensity forecast projected Katrina as a major hurricane until final landfall. The forecast discussion noted an above average level of confidence in the forecast.

At 11 a.m. EDT August 27, NHC issued a hurricane watch from Morgan City, Louisiana to the mouth of the Pearl River (Louisiana-Mississippi border), including metropolitan New Orleans. Later that afternoon, NHC extended the hurricane watch eastward across southern Mississippi to the Alabama-Florida border. On the night of August 27, TPC/NHC replaced the hurricane watch with a hurricane warning. During the next two days, only minor track adjustments were made. Meanwhile, the intensity forecast called for Katrina to be a major hurricane at landfall.

NHC introduced storm surge forecasts for southeast Louisiana and coastal Mississippi in the 11 p.m. EDT, August 27 forecasts – 32 hours prior to Katrina's landfall in southeast Louisiana. The initial storm surge forecasts were 15 to 20 feet to locally as high as 25 feet. By 10 a.m. CDT, August 28, the storm surge values were increased to a

14

range of 18 to 22 feet to locally as high as 28 feet. At this time, NHC also began emphasizing that "*preparations to protect life and property should be rushed to completion.*"

Also on August 28, NHC headlined its public advisories with the phrase "*Potentially Catastrophic*" or "*Extremely Dangerous*" to highlight the threat posed by Katrina. Comparisons were made to Hurricane Camille, the hurricane of record for the central Gulf coast, but emphasized that Katrina was a larger hurricane and its effects would be felt throughout the hurricane warning area. Concurrently, NHC activated their media pool. Despite the national media's primary focus on the potential impacts of Katrina on New Orleans, NHC personnel took every opportunity to mention that Katrina would also have a significant impact on the coast of Mississippi.

The TPC/NHC advisory issued at 4 p.m. CDT indicated the potential for the levees surrounding New Orleans to be overtopped:

> COASTAL STORM SURGE FLOODING OF 18 TO 22 FEET ABOVE NORMAL
> TIDE LEVELS...LOCALLY AS HIGH AS 28 FEET...ALONG WITH LARGE AND
> DANGEROUS BATTERING WAVES...CAN BE EXPECTED NEAR AND TO THE
> EAST OF WHERE THE CENTER MAKES LANDFALL. SOME LEVEES IN THE
> GREATER NEW ORLEANS AREA COULD BE OVERTOPPED

Katrina made landfall during the early morning of August 29 in southeast Louisiana, just south of Buras, as a strong Category 3 hurricane with estimated maximum sustained winds near 125 mph. The NHC track brought Katrina to the Louisiana-Mississippi border for its second Gulf landfall a few hours later, also as a Category 3 hurricane. NHC downgraded Katrina to a tropical storm that evening as the storm moved inland through the lower Mississippi River Valley. Katrina weakened to a tropical depression near Clarksville, TN, around 7 a.m. CDT, August 30. Later that day, TPC/NHC passed forecast responsibility for Katrina to HPC.

Florida Weather Forecast Offices

WFO Miami and WFO Key West provided a steady flow of information in the form of briefings, discussions, forecast products, watches, warnings, and statements as Katrina moved over southern Florida.

Due to a more southerly track than initially forecast, Katrina produced an estimated storm surge of three to five feet along the southwestern Florida coast of mainland Monroe County early on August 26. WFO Miami issued frequent Hurricane Local Statements (HLSs) to convey expected conditions and impacts of Katrina on South Florida, including the slight southwesterly shift in the storm's track on the 25th. The WFO Miami HLS issued at 11 p.m. EDT August 25 indicated a possible two to four foot storm surge. Approximately four to six hours later, three to five foot storm surge flooding occurred along the southwestern Florida coast.

The impact of the storm surge was especially significant in Everglades National Park: six trailers were significantly damaged and one destroyed, water damaged the lower level of ranger living quarters, seven personal vehicles flooded, eleven government vehicles flooded, and a marine store flooded. Everglades National Park officials received NWS forecasts via NOAA Weather Radio All Hazards (NWR) and the Internet.

As the forecast track of Katrina increased the threat of strong tropical storm and possibly hurricane force winds in the Keys, WFO Key West began hourly issuances of Special Weather Statements and two-hourly HLSs. These products contained specific and detailed information on the overall position of Katrina and the individual rain bands producing torrential rain and wind gusts.

At 4:45 a.m. EDT August 26, a tornado touched down in Marathon damaging a hanger and eleven aircraft at the airport. Two homes in the area were also damaged. No warning was issued for this tornado; however, the HLS in effect mentioned tornadoes were possible in the outer rain bands of Katrina. As Katrina moved west just north of the Keys, tropical rain bands remained over the middle and lower Keys producing as much as 10 inches of rain by midnight on August 27. A Flood Watch had been issued on the 24th in anticipation of the flooding. WFO Key West issued flood warnings covering the heavy rain and flooding threat.

Gulf Coast Weather Forecast Offices

WFO New Orleans/Baton Rouge, LA

Located in Slidell, LA, the WFO New Orleans/Baton Rouge service area is one of the most hurricane-prone regions of the U.S. The mean return period for a major hurricane in the New Orleans area is 19 years, one of the most frequent along the U.S. Gulf and Atlantic coastline. The area is also vulnerable to significant/catastrophic storm surge, characterized by extensive low-lying terrain. Of the 2.9 million residents within the WFO New Orleans/Baton Rouge service area, about 46 percent live either behind the levee system or in a hurricane-prone flood zone. Moreover, long lead times, about 48 to 72 hours, are required to evacuate the at-risk portion of the population.

WFO New Orleans/Baton Rouge was well prepared for Katrina. They conducted a comprehensive annual tropical cyclone training program to prepare for potential hurricane operations. In addition, they performed an office evacuation, communications, and power failure drill on August 10.

WFO New Orleans/Baton Rouge initially mentioned the system that would evolve into Katrina in their local Area Forecast Discussion during the afternoon of August 22. On August 26, WFO New Orleans/Baton Rouge contacted emergency managers in southeast Louisiana and coastal Mississippi to advise them to monitor Katrina. While they explained the uncertainty inherent in two and three day tropical cyclone forecasts, they noted the westward computer model trends and that Katrina could be a major hurricane at landfall – Category 3 or 4. They told them to prepare for potential hurricane watches and warnings the following day. Later that afternoon, the first Southeast Louisiana Hurricane Task Force (hereafter referred to as the Task Force) conference call was held. Task Force conference calls are organized and directed by the Louisiana Homeland Security Operations Center (LHSOC).

At 10 a.m. CDT August 27, NHC issued a hurricane watch for southeast Louisiana, including metropolitan New Orleans. (All references henceforth in this section are in CDT.) Accordingly, WFO New Orleans/Baton Rouge issued its first HLS for Katrina, which mentioned that while some uncertainty remained about the exact landfall location, the storm surge threat would be significant – up to 18 feet.

August 27 was a pivotal day for coordination, operations, and facility preparation. The office reviewed its hurricane staffing and operations plan, developed an operations schedule, and an additional forecaster from WFO Melbourne, FL, was brought in to assist with operations during Katrina. The office also finalized its facility preparations in coordination with the Lower Mississippi River Forecast Center (LMRFC) by topping off the generator fuel tanks, purchasing additional food, and obtaining cots. Meanwhile, the WFO management team led the coordination effort with area emergency managers and decision-makers.

By the evening of August 27, confidence was increasing on the landfall area, and TPC/NHC posted a hurricane warning that included southeast Louisiana and coastal Mississippi. The HLS issued at 10:30 p.m. emphasized the increasing likelihood of a significant hurricane landfall with storm surge of 15 to 20 feet possible.

The HLS issued at 4 a.m. August 28 highlighted the potential storm surge impacts to motivate residents in coastal sections of southeast Louisiana and Mississippi to heed the advice of local emergency management officials. It indicated storm surge potential of up to 25 feet.

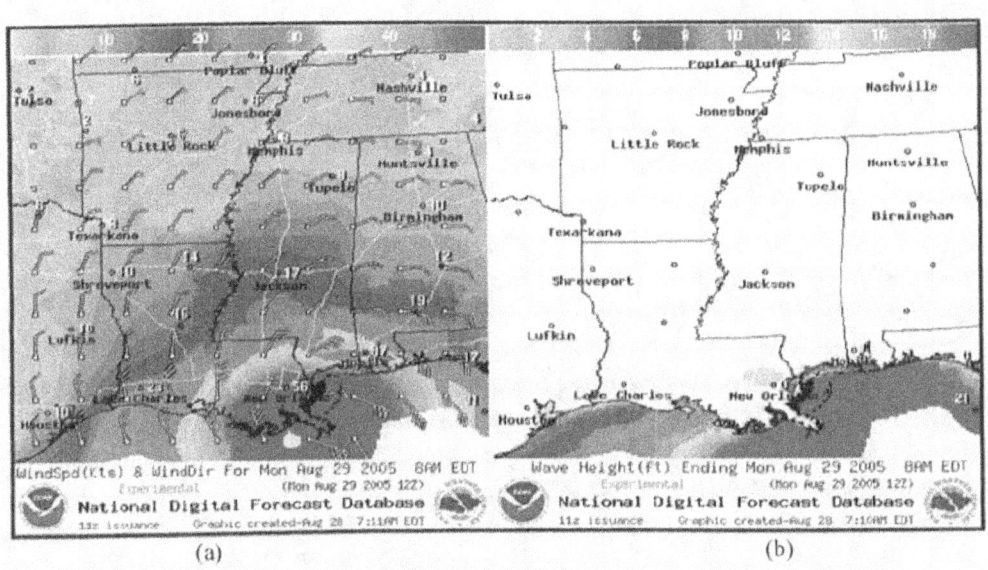

Figure 9. Snapshot of experimental NDFD gridded forecasts of (a) wind speed, wind direction, and (b) wave heights for the north Gulf coast region issued at 6 a.m., August 28, and valid at 7 a.m., August 29 – about 24 hours prior to landfall.

Figure 9 shows a snapshot of National Digital Forecast Database (NDFD) experimental gridded forecasts of wind speed, wind direction, and wave heights for the north Gulf Coast region issued at 6 a.m. August 28 and valid the following morning shortly after landfall. The gridded forecasts are well coordinated and consistent with official NWS and TPC/NHC forecasts.

Later on the morning of August 28, WFO New Orleans/Baton Rouge headlined the HLS with *"catastrophic hurricane expected"* and urged residents to rush all protective measures to completion. At 10:11 a.m., August 28, WFO New Orleans/Baton Rouge issued a statement along with its update to the inland hurricane warning that emphasized the horrific impacts Katrina would likely create for southeast Louisiana and coastal Mississippi **(Figure 10)**.

```
URGENT - WEATHER MESSAGE
NATIONAL WEATHER SERVICE NEW ORLEANS LA
1011 A.M. CDT SUN AUG 28 2005

...DEVASTATING DAMAGE EXPECTED...

.HURRICANE KATRINA...A MOST POWERFUL HURRICANE WITH UNPRECEDENTED
STRENGTH...RIVALING THE INTENSITY OF HURRICANE CAMILLE OF 1969.

MOST OF THE AREA WILL BE UNINHABITABLE FOR WEEKS...PERHAPS LONGER. AT
LEAST ONE HALF OF WELL CONSTRUCTED HOMES WILL HAVE ROOF AND WALL
FAILURE. ALL GABLED ROOFS WILL FAIL...LEAVING THOSE HOMES SEVERELY
DAMAGED OR DESTROYED.

THE MAJORITY OF INDUSTRIAL BUILDINGS WILL BECOME NON FUNCTIONAL.
PARTIAL TO COMPLETE WALL AND ROOF FAILURE IS EXPECTED. ALL WOOD
FRAMED LOW RISING APARTMENT BUILDINGS WILL BE DESTROYED. CONCRETE
BLOCK LOW RISE APARTMENTS WILL SUSTAIN MAJOR DAMAGE...INCLUDING
SOME WALL AND ROOF FAILURE.

HIGH RISE OFFICE AND APARTMENT BUILDINGS WILL SWAY DANGEROUSLY...A
FEW TO THE POINT OF TOTAL COLLAPSE. ALL WINDOWS WILL BLOW OUT.

AIRBORNE DEBRIS WILL BE WIDESPREAD...AND MAY INCLUDE HEAVY ITEMS SUCH
AS HOUSEHOLD APPLIANCES AND EVEN LIGHT VEHICLES. SPORT UTILITY
VEHICLES AND LIGHT TRUCKS WILL BE MOVED. THE BLOWN DEBRIS WILL
CREATE ADDITIONAL DESTRUCTION. PERSONS...PETS...AND LIVESTOCK EXPOSED
TO THE WINDS WILL FACE CERTAIN DEATH IF STRUCK.

POWER OUTAGES WILL LAST FOR WEEKS...AS MOST POWER POLES WILL BE DOWN
AND TRANSFORMERS DESTROYED. WATER SHORTAGES WILL MAKE HUMAN
SUFFERING INCREDIBLE BY MODERN STANDARDS.

THE VAST MAJORITY OF NATIVE TREES WILL BE SNAPPED OR UPROOTED. ONLY
THE HEARTIEST WILL REMAIN STANDING...BUT BE TOTALLY DEFOLIATED. FEW
CROPS WILL REMAIN. LIVESTOCK LEFT EXPOSED TO THE WINDS WILL BE KILLED.

AN INLAND HURRICANE WIND WARNING IS ISSUED WHEN SUSTAINED WINDS NEAR
HURRICANE FORCE...OR FREQUENT GUSTS AT OR ABOVE HURRICANE
FORCE...ARE CERTAIN WITHIN THE NEXT 12 TO 24 HOURS.
ONCE TROPICAL STORM AND HURRICANE FORCE WINDS ONSET...DO NOT
VENTURE OUTSIDE!
```

Figure 10. Inland Hurricane Warning issued by the WFO New Orleans/Baton Rouge.

This statement became a significant moment for the NWS during Katrina. The language helped reinforce the message from emergency management officials for residents in southeast Louisiana and southern Mississippi to heed evacuation orders from local officials. The unprecedented, explicitly foreboding detail was also used by emergency managers, local officials, and the media to prepare the public for Katrina's impact and aftermath (**Best Practice**). The template for this statement was developed by WFO Tampa in the 1990s.

> **FINDING 1:** This statement was highly effective in reinforcing the message from emergency management for residents to rush preparations to completion and heed evacuation orders. Templates for these statements are available in an older software program (WWA) at NWS field offices but have not been transitioned to the current operational software program (GHG).

> **RECOMMENDATION 1:** NWS Headquarters should ensure templates for these statements that emphasize potential impacts following major hurricane landfalls are available in operational software at appropriate NWS field offices. The templates should be pre-coordinated with local emergency managers.

At 11 a.m. on August 28, the Mayor of New Orleans declared a state of emergency and ordered the first-ever mandatory evacuation of the city. In addition, the mayor opened the Superdome as a shelter for those unable to evacuate the city. Meanwhile, WFO New Orleans/Baton Rouge continued to ramp up coordination activities with emergency managers and local officials.

Overnight on August 28, WFO New Orleans/Baton Rouge began issuing hourly short-term forecasts to provide information on the location of Katrina along with wind and rainfall information. At 5:27 a.m., August 29, WFO New Orleans/Baton Rouge issued its first Extreme Tropical Cyclone Destructive Wind Warning for Katrina. They issued three more such warnings over the next few hours as Katrina made its way north over southeast Louisiana, past New Orleans and towards southern Mississippi.

At 8:12 a.m., August 29, WFO New Orleans/Baton Rouge received a radio transmission from Bob Turner, Lake Borgne Levee District Manager, that the Industrial Canal levee was breached on the east side at Tennessee Street. The office promptly issued a Flash Flood Warning at 8:14 a.m. for the levee breach:

> *A LEVEE BREACH OCCURRED ALONG THE INDUSTRIAL CANAL AT TENNESSEE STREET. 3 TO 8 FEET OF WATER IS EXPECTED DUE TO THE BREACH. LOCATIONS IN THE WARNING INCLUDE BUT ARE NOT LIMITED TO ARABI AND 9TH WARD OF NEW ORLEANS. IF YOU ARE IN THE WARNING AREA MOVE TO HIGHER GROUND IMMEDIATELY.*

At 9:04 a.m. August 29, as Katrina was bearing down on Slidell and coastal Mississippi, WFO New Orleans/Baton Rouge issued a short-term forecast that provided a gust forecast for the next few hours that was consistent with the Extreme Tropical Cyclone Destructive Wind Warning:

THE EYEWALL OF KATRINA WILL MOVE ACROSS ST. TAMMANY PARISH...HANCOCK...AND HARRISON COUNTIES THIS HOUR. EXTREMELY VIOLENT WINDS OF 110 MPH WITH GUSTS TO 135 MPH WILL ACCOMPANY THE EYEWALL AS IT MOVES THROUGH. PERSONS ALONG THE GULF COAST IN THESE AREAS NEED TO TAKE SHELTER IN AN INTERIOR ROOM AS SOON AS POSSIBLE.

This was the last statement issued by WFO New Orleans/Baton Rouge before their telecommunications capabilities failed due to a widespread outage at the service provider's primary communications hub in New Orleans. WFO Mobile assumed full backup responsibility at that point.

WFO Mobile, AL

WFO Mobile has experienced more land-falling tropical cyclones than any other Gulf Coast WFO over the past 10 years. In addition to providing forecasts and warnings for their service area, WFO Mobile assumed service backup responsibility for WFO New Orleans/Baton Rouge following the communications failure. WFO Mobile did a superb job on both accounts, particularly given the fact that Hurricane Katrina directly affected the staff. Many employees suffered damage to their homes. WFO Mobile provided service backup for WFO New Orleans/Baton Rouge for 22 days.

Portions of WFO Mobile's service area experienced hurricane conditions. The maximum sustained one-minute wind speed recorded within their area was 67 mph; the highest wind gust was 84 mph. Katrina produced a storm surge of 11.5 feet in Mobile Bay, second only to the storm surge of 11.6 feet during the July 1916 hurricane. These conditions were well forecast by TPC/NHC and WFO Mobile. The first HLS was issued by WFO Mobile at 7:25 p.m. EDT August 27, about 36 hours prior to landfall. The HLS stated in part:

KATRINA IS EXPECTED TO MAKE LANDFALL SOMEWHERE NEAR SOUTHEASTERN LOUISIANA AS A MAJOR HURRICANE. WHILE EXACT LOCATION OF LANDFALL IS STILL UNCERTAIN AT THIS TIME...SIGNIFICANT AND LIFE THREATENING STORM SURGE IS EXPECTED TO BE FELT WELL EAST OF THE STORMS CENTER. BASED ON THE LATEST FORECAST TRACK...A STORM SURGE OF 8 TO 12 FEET IS EXPECTED ALONG COASTAL MOBILE COUNTY AND THE WESTERN PORTIONS OF MOBILE BAY. A STORM SURGE OF 7 TO 9 FEET IS EXPECTED ALONG COASTAL BALDWIN COUNTY. THESE SURGE HEIGHT VALUES ARE EXPECTED TO CAUSE SIGNIFICANT INUNDATION ALONG PORTIONS OF DAUPHIN ISLAND AND FORT MORGAN PENINSULA.

WFO Jackson, MS

Within WFO Jackson's service area, the primary weather-related impact of Katrina was high winds and tornadoes. Katrina produced eleven tornadoes in WFO Jackson's service area. Of these tornadoes, two were rated F-2, and the other nine were rated F-1. The damage associated with these tornadoes was mostly fallen and uprooted trees with some minor damage to roofs and buildings. WFO Jackson's average tornado warning lead time was 16.5 minutes.

Forty-six fatalities have been attributed to Katrina in WFO Jackson's service area. In addition, 568 homes and 102 mobile homes were destroyed, and 5,851 homes suffered significant damage. The State of Mississippi estimates that about one million trees were blown down and more than one million residents in central and eastern Mississippi lost power during Katrina. Wind gusts of 80 to 110 mph were widespread in the southern and eastern portion of WFO Jackson's service area.

On August 24, WFO Jackson began to provide information on Katrina to their emergency management community. While NHC forecasts kept Katrina well east of Mississippi at this time, WFO Jackson advised emergency managers to monitor the storm. By the morning of August 27, NHC's forecast brought Katrina directly into WFO Jackson's service area. Later that day, NHC posted a hurricane watch for the north central Gulf Coast including the coast of Mississippi. WFO Jackson issued a detailed Special Weather Statement that afternoon to raise awareness and recommend preparedness activities:

> *A LARGE SWATH OF SUSTAINED WIND SPEEDS AROUND 60 MILES AN HOUR AND HIGHER...INCLUDING THE POTENTIAL FOR SUSTAINED HURRICANE FORCE WINDS IN EXCESS OF 75 MPH...WILL BE POSSIBLE OVER AREAS EAST OF INTERSTATE 55 AND SOUTH OF INTERSTATE 20 MONDAY EVENING AND MONDAY NIGHT. DECIDE WHICH PART OF YOUR HOUSE IS SAFEST AND CREATE A FAMILY DISASTER PLAN. CHECK YOUR STOCK OF CANNED FOODS...FIRST AID SUPPLIES...DRINKING WATER AND PRESCRIPTION DRUGS. MAKE PLANS FOR POSSIBLE PROLONGED POWER OUTAGES AND LOSS OF WATER OR OTHER UTILITIES.*

On August 28, WFO Jackson issued inland hurricane and tropical storm watches and warnings. Their forecasts, warnings, and statements issued throughout the weekend stressed the potential for Katrina to produce significant wind damage well inland and tornadoes. Jeff Mayo, Director of Neshoba County, MS, Emergency Management Agency said as a result of the threats mentioned in the WFO Jackson forecasts, warnings, and statements, the county recommended residents leave mobile homes before the morning of August 29. A number of mobile homes were destroyed by tornadoes in Neshoba County August 29. Jeff Mayo stated that because of the county's action, based on information provided by WFO Jackson, "...*undoubtedly lives were saved.*"

On the morning of August 29, as Katrina was making landfall in southeast Louisiana, WFO Jackson shifted its focus to short-term warnings, forecasts, and statements such as the following Special Weather Statement issued at 9:25 a.m. CDT:

> *ANALYSIS OF DOPPLER RADAR AND SATELLITE IMAGERY INDICATES THAT THE NORTH SIDE OF THE DANGEROUS EYEWALL OF KATRINA WILL LIKELY BE REACHING THE SOUTHERN SECTIONS OF THESE COUNTIES BY AROUND MIDDAY.KATRINA MAY STILL BE A CATEGORY THREE HURRICANE ....WITH WINDS OF 100 TO 120 MPH POSSIBLE. THIS WOULD RESULT IN POTENTIALLY CATASTROPHIC WIND DAMAGE. TREAT THIS SITUATION AS*

IF IT WERE A TORNADO. MOVE TO AN INTERIOR ROOM OF THE LOWEST
FLOOR OF YOUR HOME OR BUSINESS.

WFO Jackson issued a total of 98 watches, warnings, and statements for Katrina.

Extreme Destructive Wind Warnings

The 2005 Atlantic hurricane season marked the organizational implementation of issuing Extreme Tropical Cyclone Destructive Wind Warnings using the Tornado Warning identifier (TOR). The warning takes advantage of the rapid dissemination of the TOR product to alert the public to the imminent passage of the eyewall of a major hurricane. The Extreme Tropical Cyclone Destructive Wind Warning advises residents to take shelter immediately in an interior portion of a well-built structure. Use of the TOR product for this purpose was identified as a best practice during the 2004 hurricane season.

Nineteen Extreme Tropical Cyclone Destructive Wind Warnings were issued during Katrina: 11 in WFO Jackson's service area and eight in WFO New Orleans/Baton Rouge's service area. A review of these warnings shows the warning headline varied, often from one issuance to another:

- *TORNADO WARNING FOR EXTREME WINDS OVER 100 MPH...*
- *TORNADO WARNING FOR CATASTROPHIC WINDS FOR...*
- *TORNADO WARNING FOR THE EYEWALL OF HURRICANE KATRINA FOR...*
- *TORNADO WARNING FOR...*

The lack of a standard headline could cause confusion among the public and our partners. In a number of issuances, the format of the Extreme Tropical Cyclone Destructive Wind Warnings was also not consistent with NWS policy.

The feedback from users and partners regarding the usefulness of this new warning was mixed. Most thought the Extreme Tropical Cyclone Destructive Wind Warnings were useful and valuable in terms of providing timely detail and appropriate information on protective action. Some broadcasters, however, pointed out specific cases where the use of the TOR identifier for multiple threats presents the potential for confusion. In one case during Katrina, a Tornado Warning was in effect north of Meridian, while a TOR for Extreme Tropical Cyclone Destructive Winds was issued south of Meridian. This made it difficult for broadcasters to display and explain the difference.

The NWS is currently working to develop a separate dissemination code for Extreme Tropical Cyclone Destructive Wind Warnings; however, it will take a minimum of three years to obtain an Emergency Alert System (EAS) identifier. In the meantime, format changes will be made to the product (issued under TOR identifier) used for Extreme Tropical Cyclone Destructive Winds to alleviate confusion where possible.

There was another problem with the Extreme Tropical Destructive Wind Warnings with regard to the language contained in the product. The standard advice template given in warnings for extreme winds is for people to take shelter in "an interior room of the lowest floor" of a building. During Hurricane Katrina, these warnings were issued for counties also at risk for storm surge flooding. HLSs describing the potential flooding hazard called for people to go to the highest floor of a building. The potential for issuing conflicting advice in these different warning products has been addressed for the 2006 hurricane season.

> **FINDING 2:** Feedback from customers and partners indicates that while the Extreme Tropical Cyclone Destructive Wind Warnings issued during Katrina were useful, the issuance under the TOR code and inconsistent product format/language caused confusion.

> **RECOMMENDATION 2A:** The NWS should implement a separate code for Extreme Tropical Cyclone Destructive Wind Warnings and a standardized product template.

> **RECOMMENDATION 2B:** The NWS should develop and distribute a one page outreach fact sheet describing Extreme Tropical Cyclone Destructive Wind Warnings to WFOs in tropical cyclone prone areas. WFOs should use this information to educate partners and users.

OPERATIONS COORDINATION

TPC/NHC began operational, real-time Sea Lake and Overland Surge from Hurricanes (SLOSH) storm surge runs for Katrina's landfall in southeast Louisiana and coastal Mississippi on August 28. **Figure 11** shows the SLOSH storm surge projection for Katrina based on the 7 a.m. CDT August 28 NHC forecast.

Personnel from the TPC Storm Surge Unit provided the real-time support for these runs and made the data available to NWS field offices via the TPC/NHC FTP server (**Best Practice**). Typically, but not always, TPC/NHC notified NWS field offices when SLOSH runs were completed and available during Hurricane Hotline conference calls.

> *"The Mobile office used IM (Instant Messenger) to get the SLOSH out to the TV stations. I think that saved a lot of lives. They do a tremendous job. I can't say enough good things about them."*
> – David Glenn, WPMI-TV NBC 15, Mobile, AL

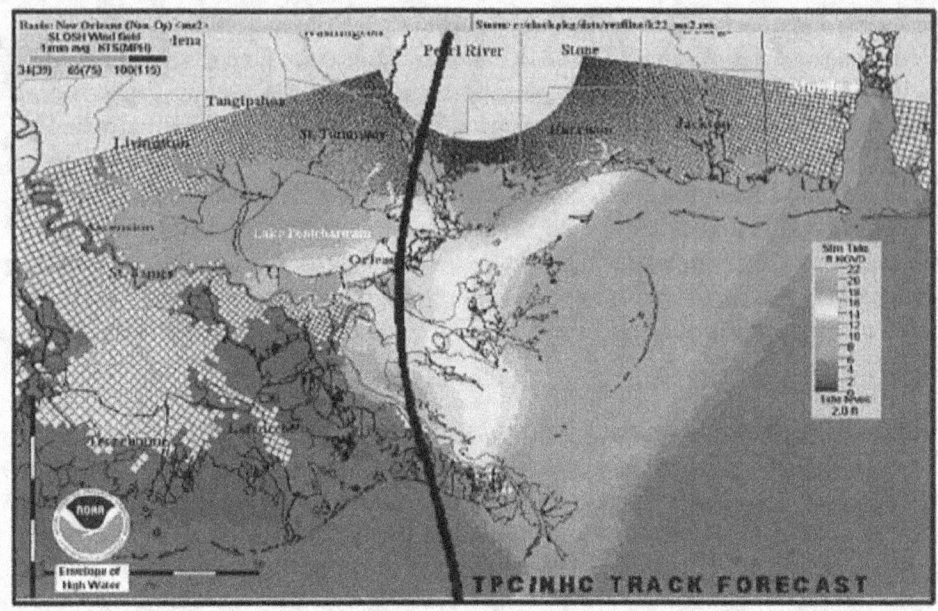

Figure 11. SLOSH storm surge data posted by TPC/NHC at 9:20 a.m. CDT, August 28, 2005 for Katrina based on 7 a.m. CDT, August 28 forecast track (denoted by black line). Graphic shows the envelope of high water relative to mean sea level (NGVD 1929). Maximum surge values of 22 feet are shown in portions of Hancock and Harrison County, Mississippi.

FINDING 3: There is no process in place to notify NWS field offices when the results from operational SLOSH storm surge runs are posted on their anonymous FTP server.

RECOMMENDATION 3A: TPC/NHC should provide notification to NWS field offices when the results from operational SLOSH storm surge runs are available on their anonymous FTP server.

RECOMMENDATION 3B: TPC/NHC should include a disclaimer statement on all operational SLOSH storm surge output made available through the anonymous FTP server that the information is for guidance purposes only and customers should refer to official NWS forecasts for official storm surge information.

On the evening of August 27, Max Mayfield, Director of NHC, contacted the Governor of Louisiana, the Governor of Mississippi, the Mayor of New Orleans, and the Alabama Emergency Management Agency to emphasize the severity of Katrina and its potential to cause a large loss of life (**Best Practice**). These calls had a profound effect on these officials and each mentioned it the following day during various press conferences. The following morning, the Mayor of New Orleans declared a state of emergency and ordered the first-ever mandatory evacuation of the city. These calls were coordinated with the HLT, but the local WFOs were not aware of the coordination.

During Katrina, the Senior Duty Meteorologist (SDM) at NCEP's Central Operations received calls from the NOAA Liaison Desk at the Department of Homeland Security's (DHS) Homeland Security Operations Center (HSOC) requesting to be connected to the NWS Hurricane Hotline conference calls. The NWS Hurricane Hotline is a secure line for internal tropical cyclone forecast coordination/collaboration among NWS field offices, NHC, other NCEP service centers, NASA, and the Department of Defense (DOD). On August 29, the SDM re-routed DHS HSOC calls for Hurricane Hotline connection from the main SDM access number to an alternate extension to keep the primary SDM number available for field support. On August 30, the SDM configured a communications bridge to allow DHS HSOC direct access to the Hurricane Hotline.

Management at the National Data Buoy Center (NDBC) also expressed a desire to participate on TPC/NHC Hurricane Hotline calls after Katrina. The interaction would provide NDBC with the opportunity to share information regarding the status of buoys within the area of tropical cyclones and other data issues with the NWS operational forecasting community. It would also help them in planning their resource management during tropical cyclone events.

FINDING 4: NDBC would benefit from participating in and could also contribute to the usefulness of the Hurricane Hotline coordination calls.

RECOMMENDATION 4: The NDBC should have access to the Hurricane Hotline.

WFO Key West uses the HURRTRAK software in their operations to coordinate with local emergency management. During Katrina, the office encountered difficulties using the automated E-mail feature in the HURRTRAK program. The problem was traced to a recent anti-virus software upgrade. As a result of the upgrade, the anti-virus software disabled the automatic e-mail feature which is used by WFO Key West to send messages to local officials from the HURRTRAK software. This made it more difficult to send information out, and required more manual effort to support its emergency management community.

FINDING 5: Anti-virus software for field office personal computers is remotely managed. HURRTRAK was not included in the anti-virus software database as an approved application. As result, the automated E-mail feature in HURRTRAK did not function, requiring manual intervention.

RECOMMENDATION 5: NWS field offices and associated regional offices should jointly review the specifications of operational PC-based software periodically to ensure network parameters are set to allow full functionality.

For its Mississippi counties, WFO New Orleans/Baton Rouge worked with the Mississippi Emergency Management Agency (MEMA) to organize and schedule conference calls. Call participants included MEMA, emergency management officials

25

from the three coastal Mississippi counties, and, at times, county and local officials. WFO New Orleans/Baton Rouge participated in six MEMA conference calls focusing on the wind, storm surge, and rainfall threat associated with Katrina. The last MEMA conference call was held at 7:15 a.m. CDT August 29.

FINDING 6: All Mississippi emergency managers contacted by the assessment team said that conference calls with NWS field offices during Katrina were of great value. However, they noted that scheduling the myriad of calls was a challenge. In addition, some emergency managers noted difficulties in prioritizing information when calls included a large number of participants.

RECOMMENDATION 6: NWS field offices should work with their state and county/parish emergency management agencies to develop conference call schedules and strategies that streamline information exchange during tropical cyclone events.

CONTINUITY OF OPERATIONS

NWS Weather Forecast Offices

Between 8 and 9 a.m. CDT August 29, shortly after the eye of Hurricane Katrina moved across the area, a massive communications failure in New Orleans resulted in cascading outages across southeast Louisiana and southern Mississippi. The flooding of New Orleans prevented industry technicians from gaining access to many sites needing repairs or fuel for backup generators to support the systems, so the outage lasted for days instead of hours. The outages affected the devices used by first responders and critical infrastructure throughout the region upon which most NWS communications and dissemination capabilities depend.

FINDING 7A: The Advanced Weather Information Processing System (AWIPS) and regional wide area network (WAN) communication failure affected primary and secondary service backup offices. This was due to a single point of failure at the service provider's primary communication hub in New Orleans, Louisiana.

FINDING 7B: WSR-88D radar communication capability at WFO Jackson and WFO New Orleans/Baton Rouge remained operational during the communications outage, but the connection to AWIPS was lost. Archive radar data was also lost.

RECOMMENDATION 7: The NWS should work closely with the various telecommunication service providers in evaluating their existing commercial telecommunication system configuration for potential single points of failure. Subsequently, the NWS should seek the assistance of the service providers in developing an alternative telecommunication network configuration that better supports field office service backup operations and requirements.

Due to the broad geographic extent and duration of the communications outage, NWS offices across the region were forced into an unprecedented service backup situation involving offices from Fort Worth to Memphis to Tallahassee. Offices that took over service responsibility for those directly in Katrina's path also invoked secondary service backup plans to manage workload. For example, WFO Tallahassee assumed responsibility for WFO Mobile's NDFD gridded forecast database while WFO Mobile covered WFO New Orleans' service area. When feasible, back up offices should be outside of the impact areas of the storm to preclude secondary backup operations. Even so, the NWS backup plans worked well, and the service responsibility changes were mostly transparent to users. A few deficiencies, particularly with regard to digital and Internet services, were noted. **Table 3** shows the duration of service back up activities at the offices impacted by Katrina.

PRIMARY OFFICE	OFFICES PROVIDING BACK UP SERVICES	DURATION OF BACK UP ACTIVITY
WFO New Orleans/ Baton Rouge	WFO Mobile, WFO Birmingham	22 days
WFO Lake Charles	WFO Houston/Galveston	13 days
WFO Jackson	WFO Huntsville	17 days
WFO Mobile	WFO Tallahassee	5 days
Lower Mississippi RFC	WFO Jackson, WFO Memphis, West Gulf RFC	16 days

Table 3. Service back up relationships and duration for WFOs and RFCs affected by Katrina.

WFO Houston/Galveston began backup operations for WFO Lake Charles shortly after Hurricane Katrina made landfall, when the office lost communications in association with the failure in New Orleans. WFO Houston/Galveston provided service backup using their personnel until the evening of August 29; thereafter, WFO Lake Charles provided personnel to assist with service backup operations (**Best Practice**). WFO Lake Charles was finally back on-line on September 10, after 13 days of support from Houston.

The gridded forecasts WFO Houston/Galveston produced for the Lake Charles service area were not automatically sent to the NWS central server. As a result, the Internet NDFD forecasts (e.g., point and click) for WFO Lake Charles were not consistently updated.

FINDING 8: There is no procedure in place to automatically send backup NDFD gridded forecasts to the NWS central server. WFO Houston/ Galveston forecasters had to manually export the WFO Lake Charles NDFD gridded forecasts to the NWS central server.

RECOMMENDATION 8: The NWS needs to develop procedures to allow WFOs providing service backup to automatically export backup NDFD gridded forecasts to the NWS central server to maintain consistent, up-to-date forecasts on the Internet.

WFO Huntsville assumed full service backup responsibility for WFO Jackson. For about the first 72 hours of backup operations, the WFO Jackson Internet page was not updated. WFO Internet websites are updated automatically whenever new forecasts are issued. However, locally unique products are not updated automatically. In addition, sections such as "Top News," which are found on every NWS local website, may need updating during extreme or rapidly evolving events to ensure up-to-date information is featured. WFO Huntsville did not initially have access to the WFO Jackson Internet site so they could not update localized WFO Jackson Internet-based products.

Once the initial communications challenges were overcome, local WFO web pages became a valuable source of response information. WFO Birmingham took the initiative to help distribute emergency information in the aftermath of Katrina, including emergency information from the Red Cross and FEMA, as well as links for locating missing family members. They disseminated this information on their Internet website, NWR, and on WFO New Orleans/Baton Rouge's website.

FINDING 9: WFO Huntsville did not have access privileges to WFO Jackson's Internet page during service backup operations.

RECOMMENDATON 9: Service backup plans need to address access to local systems and programs of the impacted office to permit updating of non-automated products and information on the office's webpages (e.g. Top News).

Terrestrial phone communications systems were unreliable due to overloading or inoperative due to damage across southeast Louisiana and southern Mississippi. Cell phones were used with some success, but cellular service was also subject to overloaded circuits. Despite the challenges, WFOs took advantage of every means at their disposal to communicate and coordinate services to support the NWS mission to protect lives and property. For example, as WFO Huntsville took over service backup for WFO Jackson, the staff at the Jackson office maintained a satellite Internet connection to use Instant Messaging to provide information to their local media partners and was still able to disseminate information on NWR. They also coordinated on tornado warnings with WFO Huntsville via cell phone. This was critical because WFO Huntsville did not have access to Jackson's WSR-88D radar data.

When WFO Mobile assumed backup responsibility for WFO New Orleans/Baton Rouge, they could not contact the office to get information. Southern Region Headquarters (SRH) had detailed a liaison to the Louisiana State Emergency Operations Center (LEOC) in Baton Rouge prior to the Katrina landfall to provide a conduit between the NWS and the State of Louisiana. However, WFO Mobile was initially unaware of this. Once communications were established with the NWS LEOC liaison, coordination ran smoothly.

In addition to the loss of commercial power in southeast Louisiana, local two-meter amateur radio repeaters were inoperative. However, High Frequency (HF) amateur radio equipment at WFO New Orleans/Baton Rouge and the Regional Operations Center (ROC) allowed them to communicate with emergency management agencies and other NWS offices during the outages. SRH sent a satellite phone to WFO New Orleans/Baton Rouge and LMRFC prior to Katrina's landfall, but due to the evacuation activities in the New Orleans area, it did not arrive until after the hurricane moved through.

FINDING 10: Critical communications activities between offices were dependent on cell phones and HF amateur radio equipment. Satellite phones were not immediately available as a communications alternative.

RECOMMENDATION 10: The NWS should identify and procure an alternative communications systems, such as HF amateur radio equipment, for its field offices. Alternate communications devices should be coordinated with emergency management agencies to ensure compatibility and inclusion in emergency operations plans.

A key challenge faced during service backup operations was the lack of ground truth observations. Data transmission and/or operation of most of the Automated Surface Observing Systems (ASOS) were disrupted due to the loss of commercial power, damage to one or more sensors, or complete destruction of the unit. This is a consistent occurrence during land-falling tropical cyclones, and has been documented in previous Service Assessments.

FINDING 11: The loss of valuable real-time ASOS data during Katrina significantly impacted the field offices' ability to assess the severity of storm-related threats and evaluate the accuracy of NWS tropical storm forecasts, and caused a break in the climate record. This finding is consistent with past tropical cyclone service assessments.

RECOMMENDATION 11: The NWS should accelerate efforts to develop viable backup power and communications capabilities and install wind sensors able to survive major hurricane winds for ASOS units, especially in coastal areas.

NWS offices anticipate and prepare to engage in service backup operations during events such as hurricanes. For example, as part of their 2005 professional development plan, WFO Huntsville developed a five-hour Weather Event Simulator training module to simulate a backup scenario for WFO Jackson during a warning situation (**Best Practice**). Then, as Hurricane Katrina approached, WFO Huntsville configured one of their AWIPS workstations to be ready for backing up WFO Jackson to ensure a smooth transition to service backup in case WFO Jackson lost communications.

To provide some perspective on the breadth of these efforts, WFO Huntsville issued 197 forecasts, warnings, and advisories for WFO Jackson during the first 48 hours of backup operations, many of which were issued as Katrina's eye passed through the WFO Jackson service area. The SAT found the service backup arrangements were transparent to many users:

> *"The specificity of the tornado warnings was so good that we could not tell that Jackson was in backup."*
> – Tony Mastro, Meteorologist, WJTV-TV12, Jackson, MS

The team reviewed traditional text-based forecasts issued by WFOs and the available National Digital Forecast Database (NDFD) forecasts. Only three NDFD forecast fields (maximum temperature, minimum temperature, and probability of precipitation) were archived at the National Climatic Data Center (NCDC) and available for review. Important forecast elements of the NDFD in hurricanes, such as wind speed and wave height, are experimental but are publicly available. An archive is needed to evaluate their quality and accuracy, especially since many of the official text-based products are produced from the NDFD grid forecasts.

FINDING 12: Experimental NDFD fields are not archived. Some of the NDFD elements have been in experimental status for years.

RECOMMENDATION 12: NWS Headquarters should review the data archiving requirements for the NDFD in consideration of this issue and adjust the policy to ensure experimental elements such as wave height and wind speed are archived.

Lower Mississippi River Forecast Center

The Lower Mississippi River Forecast Center (LMRFC), co-located with WFO New Orleans/Baton Rouge, provides continuous data assimilation, river basin modeling, hydrologic forecast preparation, and flash flood and headwater guidance to 18 WFOs from Mississippi and Louisiana north to Illinois. Their primary external partners are the USACE and the U.S. Geological Survey.

The LMRFC service backup plan identifies the NDBC, located at the Stennis Space Center in Mississippi, as the primary backup location. LMRFC stores its backup equipment, including specially configured laptop computers, at NDBC. The RFC laptop backup configuration allows LMRFC the flexibility to relocate to alternate NWS locations if the primary backup location is unavailable. This was the case during Katrina.

On August 28, after retrieving their backup equipment from NDBC, LMRFC set up backup operations at WFO Jackson with three personnel. While in service backup, the team at Jackson noticed that the LMRFC backup laptop did not have compatible software and data with the AWIPS-based National Headquarters Operational RFC system (NHOR).

FINDING 13: NHOR could not be fully utilized during LMRFC backup operations because the system was not compatible with the RFC backup laptops. LMRFC also had difficulties keeping the AWIPS software up-to-date on the backup laptop.

RECOMMENDATION 13A: The NHOR system needs to be configured and tested for service backup.

RECOMMENDATION 13B: Future AWIPS software upgrades for RFCs should include provisions for laptop upgrades.

When communications at WFO Jackson went down during the morning of August 29, the LMRFC relayed a message via amateur radio to transfer back up to WFO Memphis. This arrangement had been predetermined ahead of time, and the backup operations for LMRFC went smoothly at WFO Memphis. However, as the damage in the aftermath of Katrina was fully realized, it was determined that longer term back up operations should be transferred to another RFC. On September 1, the LMRFC relocated service backup operations to the West Gulf River Forecast Center (WGRFC) in Fort Worth, where it remained until September 14, 2005. The LMRFC was in service backup operations for a total of 16 days, well beyond any previous service backup event.

Feedback from WFOs in LMRFC's service area indicates that they experienced the same high level of service during backup operations they receive during normal operations. However, partners encountered some difficulties during LMRFC service backup. The USACE did not receive radar-rainfall estimates for the Ross Barnett Reservoir during service backup operations. Also, partners and users were unable to obtain routine hydrometeorological information from the LMRFC Internet site, including the Advanced Hydrologic Prediction System (AHPS).

FINDING 14: The LMRFC service backup plan does not have provisions for updating their core suite of Internet-based products, including AHPS.

RECOMMENDATION 14: RFC service backup plans must include provisions for updating the core suite of Internet-based RFC products, including AHPS.

National Data Buoy Center

The National Data Buoy Center (NDBC), located at the NASA Stennis Space Center in southwest Mississippi, designs, develops, operates, and maintains a network of nearly 150 data collecting buoys and coastal stations in the Gulf of Mexico, the Atlantic and Pacific Oceans. NDBC provides hourly observations of wind speed and direction, gusts, barometric pressure, and air temperature from their network. In addition, some platforms measure wave height. This observational data is utilized by both NCEP and WFOs to support marine and the tropical cyclone forecast and warning program.

NDBC began to monitor Hurricane Katrina on August 26. Based on the NHC track forecast that afternoon, NDBC invoked their hurricane plan, which included the immediate transfer of all materials from outside the building to an interior portion of the facility. The plan also details some personnel to the buoy maintenance building.

Overall, NDBC's hurricane plan worked well during Katrina. Prior to the storm, NASA opened the administrative building as a public hurricane shelter. The eye of Katrina passed over the NDBC facility and lasted for about 90 minutes. The building sustained moderate damage.

Due to the communications outage in New Orleans on August 29, all of NDBC's telecommunications systems failed, including their Internet and data servers. Shortly thereafter, the facility also lost commercial power, and they switched over to generator power for the next 15 days.

After the communication outage at NDBC, buoy and other marine network data continued to be received at Wallops Island, VA. This data was processed; quality controlled, and transmitted to AWIPS and other external users at NWS Headquarters (NWSH) in Silver Spring, MD. However, the NDBC staff could not intervene if there was a data problem. In addition, the NDBC backup plan had no provision for receiving or processing partner data and data from the DART (Deep-ocean Assessment and Reporting of Tsunami) buoy stations that are deployed throughout the world's oceans as part of the tsunami detection and early warning system.

> **FINDING 15:** The NDBC backup plan has no provision for Internet web page mirroring or remote collection and distribution of DART buoy data and partner data.

> **RECOMMENDATION 15:** The NDBC needs to revise its service backup plan to identify backup requirements, and associated resources, including provisions for remote collection and dissemination of buoy observations and partner data, data quality control functions, and the possible deployment of personnel to support service backup operations.

Katrina disabled three buoys and two C-MAN stations: one buoy was overturned and will need to be rebuilt; the other two buoys were adrift due to mooring failures. The two C-MAN stations were destroyed.

NDBC management expressed an interest in participating on internal TPC/NHC Hurricane Hotline conference calls for tropical cyclones. It would provide an opportunity for NDBC to share information regarding the status of buoys within the area of tropical cyclones and data issues with the NWS operational forecasting community. In addition, NDBC indicated that it would also help them manage their resources (**Recommendation 4**).

SUPPORT ACTIVITIES

Southern Region Headquarters (SRH) provides administrative, technical, and operational support for 46 NWS field offices as well as state and federal partners. SRH also operates a Regional Operations Center (ROC), which provides direct operational support to its field offices during hazardous events and coordinates event-specific information with other headquarters offices.

SRH elevated the operations status of their ROC on August 23 to provide expanded hours of operation and maintained this level of support for 29 days. The staff conducted more than 60 media interviews and issued more than 150 reports documenting the impacts of Katrina. The information provided by the ROC to NWSH, NOAA, and other government agencies was utilized to support Katrina post storm response and recovery activities.

Within a few days following the communications failure in southeast Louisiana, ROC personnel used satellite phones to communicate with field office personnel at WFO New Orleans/Baton Rouge and WFO Jackson. A few days later, HF amateur radio equipment was installed in the ROC to provide additional communications capability.

FINDING 16: SRH often received multiple, even duplicate, requests from NWSH, NOAA, and other federal agencies for information contained in Regional Operations Center impact statements, especially after Katrina's landfall in southeast Louisiana/southern Mississippi.

RECOMMENDATION 16A: The NWS should improve the process for distributing field information for various headquarters elements of NOAA/NWS and other federal agencies in order to eliminate duplication and streamline the exchange of information during significant events.

RECOMMENDATION 16B: NOAA/NWS needs to clearly define the roles, responsibilities and expectations of the NOAA Interagency Coordination Center (NICC), the NOAA/NWS liaison desk at the DHS HSOC, the NWS Awareness Branch, and the NWS Regional Headquarters, in order to make the exchange of information more efficient and effective during significant events.

The support effort of NWS Incident Meteorologists (IMET) was substantial and successful during Katrina. IMETs provide tactical and logistical weather information in support of a mission such as clean up efforts after a major weather related disaster. In the aftermath of Hurricane Katrina, nine certified IMETs and two trainees were deployed to support operations at the Louisiana EOC, WFO New Orleans/Baton Rouge, Stennis Space Center, and downtown New Orleans.

The IMETs were deployed for nearly 120 days after Katrina, working in 16 hour shifts. They maintained a weather watch and provided forecasts in support of the recovery operations, established Internet communications to WFO New Orleans/Baton Rouge, and installed five Remote Automated Weather Systems (FireRAWS) to the area. (FireRAWS are provided by the Bureau of Land Management and are usually used on wildfire incidents.) The FireRAWS were deployed along the coast to support NOAA HAZMAT operations as well as to several airports. The New Orleans International Airport's ASOS had been disabled by the hurricane, and the FireRAWS equipment enabled the airport to resume operations, especially humanitarian and rescue operations **(Best Practice)**.

SRH also deployed staff to assist offices working in the field, including at the LHSOC in Baton Rouge, Louisiana. Their role was to provide hydrometeorological information to support rescue and recovery activities and to relay information from other agencies at the LHSOC to WFO New Orleans/Baton Rouge for distribution to local emergency management, including levee-related data. The LHSOC appreciated the support provided by NWS personnel during Katrina:

> *"Our relationship with the NWS works. It was great to have an NWS person here in Baton Rouge with us on the front lines."*
> – Lt. Col. William J. Doran, III, Chief of Operations, Office of Homeland Security and Emergency Preparedness, Louisiana Military Department

WFOs provided up to 22 days of service backup following Hurricane Katrina. SRH provided additional workstations to WFO Mobile and several other offices to support extended service backup operations **(Best Practice)**.

Once SRH was able to contact WFO New Orleans/Baton Rouge and the Lower Mississippi RFC following Katrina, they discovered that the impact on the area surrounding the office was catastrophic. Of the 43 staff members, 15 suffered severe damage to their homes, and five had moderate damage. Several families needed temporary housing until repairs could be made on their homes.

In response, SRH deployed two teams to assist with office restoration, home repairs, food and water, and temporary quarters. These teams transported generators, tarps, fuel, an icemaker, and other equipment to the office and obtained diesel fuel to replenish the office generators. Meanwhile, SRH was able to expedite the deployment of FEMA housing trailers to the office for emergency housing for NWS personnel. Other NWS Regions also quickly pitched-in and provided satellite phones and personnel to assist with operational recovery activities and temporary housing.

OUTREACH AND PREPAREDNESS

NWS personnel conduct a tremendous amount of tropical cyclone outreach annually, including participating in national and international conferences, leading hurricane awareness week activities, promoting hurricane education in schools, and providing training for emergency management personnel and other decision makers.

Each year, TPC/NHC hosts and provides instructors for three-week long FEMA-sponsored *Introduction to Hurricane Preparedness* courses held each year. The feedback from emergency managers in southeast Louisiana and southern Mississippi was extremely supportive of the FEMA-TPC/NHC course and identified it as an important course for all emergency managers to understand and effectively apply TPC/NHC forecasts **(Best Practice)**.

WFO New Orleans/Baton Rouge has participated in a variety of exercises and provided weather scenarios and storm surge implications, including a five-day exercise in July 2004 held at the LEOC, called "Hurricane Pam." The exercise, sponsored by FEMA and the State of Louisiana, was designed to help officials develop joint response plans for a catastrophic hurricane in Louisiana. The exercise used realistic weather information developed by WFO New Orleans/Baton Rouge. In the scenario, Hurricane Pam hit New Orleans with sustained winds of 120 mph, produced up to 20 inches of rain in parts of southeast Louisiana and created a storm surge that overtopped levees in the New Orleans area.

The Southeast Louisiana Hurricane Task Force was formed after Hurricane Andrew in 1992, composed of parish emergency managers, the LHSOC, state police, and several other officials. The goal of the Task Force was to improve hurricane preparedness and response. It provided an organized and efficient conference call process for WFO New Orleans/Baton Rouge to exchange critical forecast information with state, parish, and local emergency managers during Katrina.

According to estimates provided by the local media, approximately 80 percent of the total population of New Orleans evacuated the city prior to Katrina. Jefferson Parish Emergency Management reported that they evacuated 375,000 of their 450,000 residents – an 83 percent evacuation rate. These evacuation rates are well above the estimates from the July 2005 University of New Orleans' *Citizen Hurricane Evacuation Behavior in Southeastern Louisiana: A Twelve Parish Study*. The study concluded approximately 60 percent of the residents in southeast Louisiana would evacuate if a Category 4 or 5 hurricane threatened the area or if evacuations were recommended by local/parish emergency management officials.

The actions of WFO New Orleans/Baton Rouge leading up to Katrina's landfall, coupled with their efforts and those of the entire NWS tropical cyclone outreach program over the last two decades, contributed to timely evacuations in southeast Louisiana and coastal Mississippi and, ultimately, saved lives.

> "*The forecast for Katrina was outstanding and very accurate. We moved heavy equipment out of the risk area, and evacuated people based on the Weather Service forecasts. The Weather Service has been proactive with the Southeast Louisiana Hurricane Task Force.*"
> – Jesse St. Amant, Director, Emergency Management and President of the Southeast Louisiana Hurricane Task Force, Plaquemines Parish, LA

BEST PRACTICES

The SAT took note of several innovative actions NWS offices used to accomplish the mission. The following list contains those, which were highly successful and are appropriate for consideration at other NWS offices or in other operational scenarios.

1. The Director of TPC called the Governor of Louisiana, Governor of Mississippi, Mayor of New Orleans, and the Alabama Emergency Management Agency to underscore the severe nature of Katrina and the potential for large loss of life.

2. HPC has developed a historical rainfall database for land-falling United States tropical cyclones. HPC forecasters utilize the database during operations for historical comparisons with real-time tropical cyclones.

3. WFO Key West developed an Internet briefing tool called a Video HLS. It provides a discussion of current tropical cyclone conditions, a forecast discussion, expected impacts in their service area, and ongoing preparedness and evacuation activities in the Florida Keys.

4. WFO New Orleans/Baton Rouge issued vividly worded statements describing the likely dire impacts of Katrina and the resulting post-storm environment across southeast Louisiana and coastal Mississippi a day prior to landfall.

5. WFO Miami provides several products and services in Spanish (e.g., Spanish HLS, Spanish Internet web pages, and Spanish telephone weather forecast recordings). In addition, they provide Spanish radio/TV interviews and often assist TPC/NHC with Spanish media inquiries.

6. The entire staff at WFO Mobile has identification cards issued by the Mobile County Emergency Management Agency that allowed them to travel to and from work during the curfew imposed by local officials following Hurricane Katrina.

7. SRH provided additional workstations to WFO Mobile and other offices to support extended service backup operations.

8. When WFO Lake Charles lost communications, they proactively sent staff to WFO Houston to help provide service backup for their CWA. This transition went smoothly, at least in part, because such a scenario is practiced annually.

9. WFOs utilized Instant Messaging as an effective additional communication tool to coordinate and exchange hydrometeorological information with emergency managers and the media prior to and during Katrina.

10. WFO New Orleans/Baton Rouge and the ROC used HF amateur radio equipment to communicate with emergency management agencies and other NWS offices after commercial power and communications systems failed.

11. The emergency management directors in the New Orleans area found the FEMA Introduction to Hurricane Preparedness course, co-sponsored by TPC/NHC personnel, to be essential for effectively utilizing NWS tropical cyclone products and services during Hurricane Katrina.

12. IMETs served a critical role in the aftermath of Katrina by supporting the Louisiana EOC, the NOAA HAZMAT Team, and WFO New Orleans/Baton Rouge. They filled gaps in the weather observation network due to the storm's impacts by installing BLM's FireRAWS equipment and established a portable data reception/transmission system for use by WFO New Orleans/Baton Rouge and local officials.

13. SRH deployed two teams to help in restoration and recovery efforts of the impacted offices.

CONCLUSION

The impact of Hurricane Katrina on the Gulf Coast was tremendous. The storm surge devastated coastal Mississippi, and much of New Orleans was inundated with 15 to 20 feet of water. Katrina spread hurricane force winds well inland and spawned 62 tornadoes in eight states. The loss of life and extraordinary damage made Katrina the costliest hurricane in U.S. history and the deadliest hurricane in 77 years.

Katrina caused significant disruptions in the communication infrastructure surrounding New Orleans. NWS offices in Louisiana and Mississippi experienced communications outages, and NWS continuity of operations plans were implemented, engaging offices from Texas to Florida for service backup functions.

The SAT evaluated the effectiveness of NWS services and operational procedures with respect to this event, paying particular attention to continuity of operations procedures/plans, coordination and collaboration with emergency managers and decision-makers, and forecast and warning accuracy. The team found that the NWS performed exceptionally well before, during, and after Katrina. This was confirmed by the overwhelmingly positive feedback from users of NWS products and services. Overall, the timeliness and accuracy of NWS forecast products were well above performance standards.

Throughout the event, NWS field offices provided high quality forecast and warning information to the public, mass media, and emergency management officials. Feedback from all groups was very positive. WFO New Orleans/Baton Rouge issued a statement one day prior to Katrina's landfall that outlined the potential devastating impacts of the hurricane on southeast Louisiana and coastal Mississippi. Due to the unprecedented detail and foreboding nature of the language used, the statement helped reinforce the actions of emergency management officials as they coordinated one of the largest evacuations in U.S. history.

Service backup for offices affected by the communications outage was effective and transparent to most users and partners. However, single points of failure need to be addressed, and communication devices that do not depend on the local infrastructure should be explored. Hardware and software requirements for extended periods of service backup support also must be identified and addressed.

Problems related to the use of the Extreme Tropical Cyclone Destructive Wind Warning were uncovered and are being addressed. The potential for communicating conflicting safety information has already been addressed, and improvements to product dissemination are planned.

Appendix A

The Saffir-Simpson Hurricane Scale

The Saffir-Simpson Hurricane Scale is a 1-5 rating based on the hurricane's present intensity. This is used to give an estimate of the potential property damage and flooding expected along the coast from a hurricane landfall. Wind speed is the determining factor in the scale, as storm surge values are highly dependent on the slope of the continental shelf and the shape of the coastline in the landfall region. Note that all winds are using the one-minute average at 10 meter elevation.

CATEGORY	SUSTAINED WIND IN MPH	BAROMETRIC PRESSURE IN MILLIBARS	STORM SURGE IN FEET ABOVE NORMAL	DAMAGE
1	74-95	>980	4-5	Minimal
2	96-110	965-979	6-8	Moderate
3	111-130	945-964	9-12	Extensive
4	131-155	920-944	13-18	Extreme
5	>155	<920	>18	Catastrophic

Appendix B

Best Track Analysis for Hurricane Katrina
(courtesy of TPC/NHC)

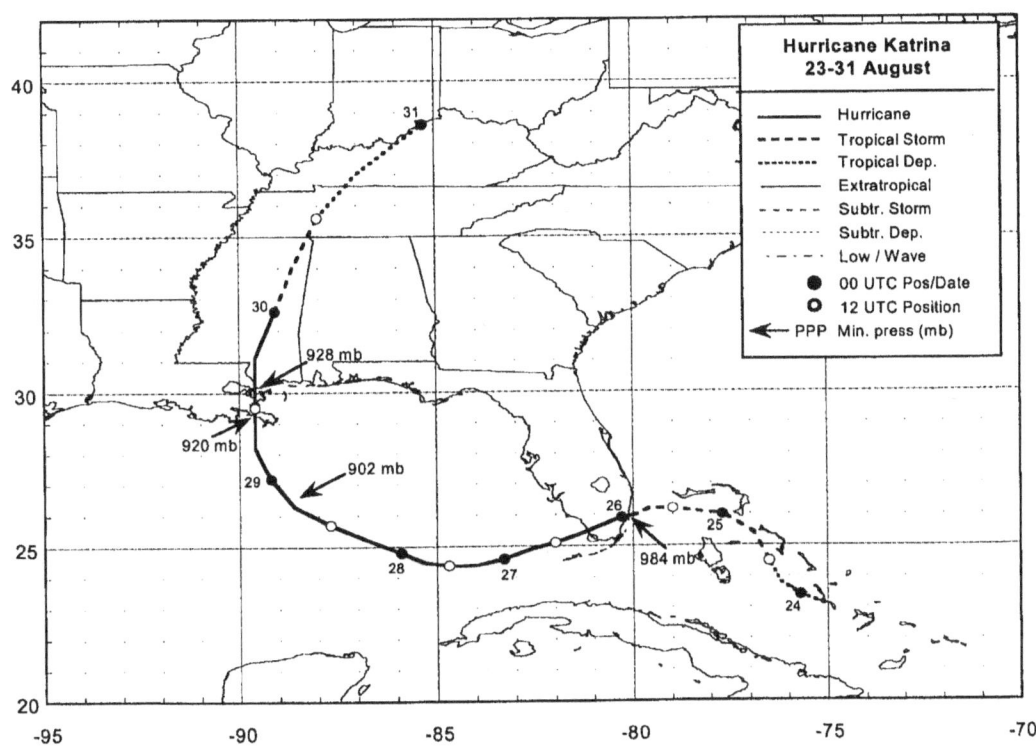

Appendix C

Tornado Reports Associated with Hurricane Katrina
(Red triangles indicate areas where tornadoes occurred)

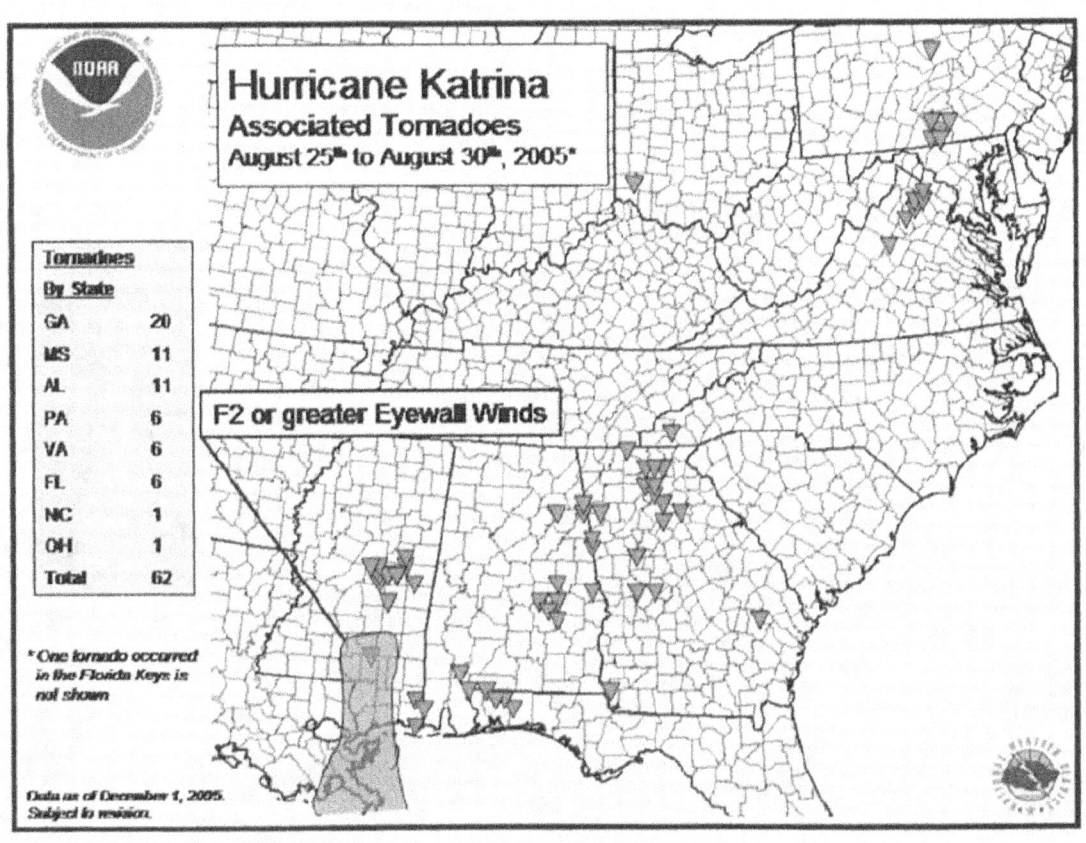